The CALL OF THE LAND

An Agrarian Primer for the 21st Century

Steven McFadden

Reviews of Steven McFadden's books:

Resurgence Magazine on Farms of Tomorrow: "It is rare to come across any practical farming guide that sets out, from its inception, a set of principles that embrace social, spiritual and economic concerns on completely equal terms...The wisdom and clarity of philosophy are striking throughout."

Whole Earth Review on Farms of Tomorrow: "This is the best book to access the Community Supported Agriculture (CSA) movement, including philosophical, spiritual, practical essays and how-to (including financial discussions). This is the source for tools, organizations, farms, and networks concerning the renewal of agriculture."

New York Times Book Review: "Profiles in Wisdom does a fine job not only of presenting the dignity, complexity, and wit of important Indian philosophers and religious leaders, but also of issuing cautions against easy uplift and wisdom injections...There are some stirring and unexpected powers unleashed in this book."

Library Journal on Profiles in Wisdom: "This wise and provocative collection is highly recommended."

The Washington Times on Profiles in Wisdom: "Our leaders should sit and listen to the counsel Steven McFadden has gathered in this book."

The CALL OF THE LAND

An Agrarian Primer for the 21st Century

Steven McFadden

NorLightsPress.com
2721 Tulip Tree Rd.
Nashville, IN 47448

Printed in the United States of America

ISBN: 978-1-935254-11-9

Cover Design by Sammie L. Justesen
Book Design by Nadene Carter

First printing, 2009

Dedication

For the next seven generations of our children

Acknowledgments

For inspiration in developing the concept for this book I thank Elizabeth Wolf and Ellen Kleiner of Blessingway. For sharing his wisdom on matters agrarian, I thank Trauger Groh, my co-author on other works. For initial belief in the project and support for writing, I thank Gibbs Smith and the staff of Gibbs Smith Publishers. For companionship through the months of research and writing, I thank Dawn Renee Abriel. For trust and persistence, I thank my agent Sammie Justesen; for faith to go ahead and publish, I thank her husband, Vorris "Dee" Justesen of NorLightsPress. For their insight and clarity, I thank the host of agrarian writers and thinkers, in particular those whose voices are woven into this volume.

Table of Contents

Introduction

"You never change anything by fighting the existing. To change something, build a new model and make the existing obsolete." ~ Buckminster Fuller ~

This is a primary book about food, land, and people — both a survey and a synthesis of visions, ethics, practices, systems, and networks that can make it possible for us to eat well and wisely, now and in the future. *The Call of the Land* demonstrates positive steps citizens, communities, churches, corporations, and farmers are taking to establish a wholesome, enduring agrarian foundation.

As a journalist I've been paying special attention to the land since the late 1970s when I worked as farm and garden columnist for a rural New Hampshire newspaper, *The Monadnock Ledger*. Since then, I've written two books on community farms and five other books concerned with the health of our Earth and our lives upon the land. I've also absorbed messages from hundreds of learned people who spoke and wrote about our world and how we draw our sustenance from it. Many things have become plain.

Food and farms are involved in a blitzkrieg of changes, and agrarian questions emerge as critical for our future. Impending matters of finance, transport, petrochemical supply, climate stability, environmental health, water supply, food availability and composition necessitate — right now — a clear, visionary look at these issues. We've begun a transition the likes of which few people are prepared for, but to which we can all respond with intelligence and skill. This volume is intended to serve as a rough guide, helping point to a general direction for our best future, and encouraging readers to dig deep and explore further.

Agriculture is the foundation of our civilization. Everything else depends on our ability to meet the primary needs of clean food and water. This state of affairs is a blessed necessity. It creates potential for our human souls to commune with the soul of the land, and thus agrarianism has potential to serve as the basis for the wholesome renewal of our overall relationship with the Earth and each other.

The economic and natural worlds are mutating around us. Inescapably and immediately, we must mobilize our will, intelligence, and strength on the essential matter of producing clean food for ourselves in a way that stabilizes and heals the land. This is the most basic and necessary idea of 21st century agrarianism.

The problems of the land belong not just to a small minority of people who are active farmers: these are problems for all humanity. Worldwide, our systems of food production and our diets are evolving at warp speed while our climate wobbles, creating a troubling prospect for land, plants, animals and, inevitably, for us. Many people recognize this, yet lack a sense of how they might respond. This book documents a range of ideas, models, and steps that lead forward.

A few farmers burdened with debt and confronting a chaotic economy and a changing climate cannot alone take care of us all. Individuals, families, and communities have an opportunity and a responsibility to step forward and be directly involved in producing an ample supply of clean food, while also helping to heal our distressed environment.

As a matter of survival, the land is calling out to us. As a matter of survival, we must listen and respond. We have the potential to do this with a wisdom that will reverberate for generations to come.

I've come to understand that agrarian philosophy is concerned with having people concentrate on the fundamental goods of the Earth; holding our land respectfully in mind as society progresses through technological innovation, social growth, and planetary change.

Agrarianism has not, by definition, embraced industrial farming, with its focus on monetary profit and its vast, concentrated scale, dependence on dwindling supplies of oil, reliance on monocultures of crops and animals, and mass experiments with genetically engineered crops and cloned animals. Agrarians seek not to conquer and subdue the land, but rather to cooperate with it for mutual benefit.

Agrarianism has a long tradition of thinkers and writers, such as Henry David Thoreau, Thomas Paine, Victor Davis Hanson, Andrew Lytle, John Crowe Ransom, Wallace Stegner, Wes Jackson, Gene Logsdon, Joel Salatin, Peggy Bartlett, Eliot Coleman, Barbara Kingsolver, Vandana Shiva, Michael Pollan, and many others.

U.S. President Thomas Jefferson was an early proponent of the agrarian ideal as a way for the immigrating peoples of the world to make a secure home in North America. What came to be known as Jeffersonian Democracy offered the vision of a nation of independent farmers providing a wholesome and stable foundation for society — a foundation of truer value than paper money — into which the rest of culture could sink steadying roots. Jefferson and others posited that agrarianism would assure virtue, morality, and mature independence in the citizens of the land, necessary ingredients for a sound democracy. But the power of Jefferson's vision dissipated. For a host of reasons, agriculturists chose another path: industrialization and commercialization.

In the 1930s, the Nashville Agrarians revived the agrarian vision with their landmark collection of essays, *I'll Take My Stand*. The writers cast an image of agrarian ideals somehow existing in opposition to industrial society, and as a way to preserve the family from the encroachments of modern mechanization and materialism. The Nashville Agrarians were criticized by some as reactionaries, defending an impossibly romantic and outdated vision of the ideal way people should live upon the land. Others praised them as having eloquently advanced a sensible vision for the present and the future.

Late in the 20th Century, Wendell Berry wrote *The Unsettling of America: Culture and Agriculture*, developing the modern context of agrarianism. He observed that industrialism is a way of thought, based on economy, onto which is appended a culture. By contrast, he wrote, agrarianism is a way of life based on the land and the culture of the people. At the same time it is an economy.

Now, early in a new millennium, circumstances continue changing. As the Earth reaches its limits, as the climate swings, and as oil becomes scarcer and more expensive, the agrarian vision again merits aggressive consideration.

* * * *

An age of extreme weather is upon us, having a profound impact on our land and food supply. In this context, along with radical economic flux, we must consider agrarianism.

Before I summarize evidence supporting climate change, I ask you to contemplate the words of the late Algonquin Indian elder, Frank Decontie. He spoke beside a roaring ceremonial fire at high noon on the shore of First Encounter Beach, Massachusetts, June 23, 1995, at the outset of an epic walk from the Atlantic to the Pacific.

"We Native people see what is going on. We see the fish are gone. We see that there are no cod any longer here on Cape Cod. We see the trees are dying. We see that the fresh waters are now bitter. We see the people suffering everywhere. We see the animals dying. We see the hole in the sky. We don't need to go into a laboratory to understand this. We see it with our eyes and with our hearts. We see what is going on."

I see it, too. Our modern, densely populated world faces climate change, acid rain, air pollution, hazardous waste disposal, erosion of topsoils, ozone depletion, smog, water pollution, desertification, rain forest destruction, and vast dead zones in the oceans created by chemical runoff from farm fields. I take this as primary evidence. And then I listen to hear the call being lifted by the world's top scientists as they make direct, careful observations of what is really happening.

Our situation has become so marked that geologists propose the addition of a new epoch to the geological time scale. They call it the "Anthropocene" — an epoch when, for the first time in Earth's history, humans become a predominant geophysical force. The new epoch name acknowledges that humans now share responsibility with natural forces for the state of our planet.

- In 2008 researchers from top scientific institutions bluntly declared "Civilization itself is threatened by global warming." Planet Earth today is in "imminent peril." Global climate change is creating conditions where agricultural production is no longer predictable or dependable. Therefore, everyone with the opportunity and the means — and that includes most of humanity — would be wise to turn attention to the land and cultivate ways to bring forth its bounty in a manner that not only supplies food, but also heals — rather than harms — our Earth.

- More than four times as many weather-related disasters have occurred in the last 30 years than in the previous 75 years, according to the Center for Research on the Epidemiology of Disasters. Scientists reckon the stronger effects of global climate change will get underway after 2009.

- The Sixth Great Mass Extinction of life is underway right now according to scientists. The world's species are declining at a rate "unprecedented since the extinction of the dinosaurs" and human behavior is to blame according to The Living Planet Index. Some scientists speak of this epidemic of extinction as *omnicide* — the killing of everything.

The status quo for our use of the land has morphed, becoming an infernal loop. Agriculture is the human activity with the single greatest impact upon the planet. As currently practiced, it's a chief source of pollution and of natural system disruption. Industrial agriculture contributes to global environmental problems, and then becomes a direct victim of their consequences.

Most of us survive on food produced with nonrenewable resources, such as petroleum. This food production system also depends upon nearly exhausted supplies of mineral phosphate, and water from ice-age aquifers that are rapidly drying up.

Based on satellite observations, the UN's Food and Agriculture Organization (FAO) reported in 2008 that about 24 percent of the world's 1.5 billion hectares of cropland are depleted. Farming methods are, in general, the cause of this suicidal cropland ruination.

The kind of toxic agriculture behind this degradation is evident in massive dead zones infesting the Gulf of Mexico and along the Pacific Northwest coast, and in toxic rivers and embittered groundwater throughout the heartland. Caused chiefly by chemical runoff from industrial use of the land, this pollution reduces our food stocks from rivers and oceans.

The UN Environment Program concluded the planet's water, land, air, plants, animals, and fish stocks are all in "inexorable decline," and evidence shows much of this decline is due to agriculture.

This is an insidious loop. Our global climate is changing because of what we're doing to the land. And as a consequence of climate shift, farm production grows less dependable.

Birds, bees, and bats continue to perish in great numbers around the world. The massive die-offs affect not only their specific communities of life, but also our natural world and food supply. Our winged relatives weave essential threads through the whole of life as they carry pollen from plant to plant and cause the land to bloom. Their loss to Earth is inestimable.

The ongoing decline of pollinators is one form of global change that will alter the shape and structure of the land and our capacity to live upon it. Researchers still don't agree why bees are dying, but among the primary suspects are chemical farming, poor management of hives, genetically modified plants and seeds, and sensory interference from microwaves and cell phones.

A tidal wave of genetic technology is upon us with far-reaching implications for agriculture. Genetically engineered crops have already spread to millions of hectares of land around the world, with scant public input on the impact of genetic engineering to the land and our health.

The technology has spread so fast that adverse and irreversible consequences may occur before we grasp the implications. These technologies tend to work against rather than for the source of the soil's fertility. Their focus is not on enhancing and strengthening life in nature, but rather on a deadened, materialistic industrial approach.

Genetic engineering doesn't address the fundamental problem of our era: enabling plants to thrive in the context of a healthy, life-enhancing relationship with the land and nature. Genetic engineering is yet another way of trying to conquer or subdue nature, rather than finding ways to cooperate.

Even if genetically modified seeds lived up to all that's promised, patents are another significant problem. Biotech companies are monopolizing seeds, actually privatizing the DNA of life. They sell the GE-seeds at many times the price of normal seeds, and along with the seeds comes a contract that must be signed, preventing farmers from collecting seeds off their own land at the end of the season. This is a fundamental rupture of humankind's historic free access to nature.

Another issue is the prevailing use of petrochemical fertilizers and pesticides, heavily processed food, and endocrine-disrupting chemicals found universally — not only in our food, but also in our air, homes, and drinking water. These foreign substances and the increasingly widespread process of irradiating foods have an unknowable impact upon the cells of our bodies.

Research shows the tissue of the average human being contains hundreds of synthetic chemicals not found in nature. According to the Harvard School of Public Health, this chemical flood leads to developmental disorders in one of every six children, and is feminizing males of every class of vertebrate animals, from fish to mammals.

As a consequence of these daunting long-term risks, I remain skeptical of genetic engineering and the associated marketing promises. We're rushing into it much too fast — with scant consideration for generations of children who'll follow us.

These multiple crises of environment, economy, and health signal the immediate need for a transformation at the deepest levels of cultural organization, throughout our planet. A UNESCO report in 2008 warned that modern farming practices and rules must change. The report said farming has caused more than a third of the world's most deteriorated land. "Business as usual is no longer an option," the report stated. UNESCO called for a worldwide paradigm shift toward sustainable agriculture.

Since our use of the land is the predominant geophysical force on our planet, could we not use the land — through an enlightened agrarianism — in ways that are not only harmless, but also positive, life-enhancing, and climate stabilizing? The implications are enormous.

To achieve this, we need to re-scale and re-structure virtually everything we do in relation to the land. This restructuring is a vast, yet inescapable undertaking, perhaps the master ecological project of our epoch. But we already possess 10,000 years of accumulated agrarian wisdom to carry us forward, if we marry the wisdom with benign, non-polluting, cutting-edge technology and systems.

The Call of the Land echoes what agrarians hear when they listen to the call of the land and then respond. This book presents models for households, communities, and the overall system of land, labor, and food production. All these possibilities can become threads as we weave a 21st Century agrarian vision for ourselves, our children, and our children's children.

The movement toward clean, local farms and food is already underway and gaining strength. Consumers in practically every city, town, and neighborhood across America are reconnecting with local farmers and artisans to create the seeds of a new agrarianism.

While no single remedy can resolve the challenges we face, many pathways lead to healing the land and creating a wholesome agrarian foundation. This book illuminates many of those paths, revealing how a sustainable agrarian foundation can serve the fragile high-tech, digital-wave culture emerging so dynamically in our world.

Chapter One
Listening to the Call

Listening is one of the oldest and most valued traditions of our land. For centuries, to listen more clearly, people have made pilgrimages to mountains, fields, forests, plains, and canyons. In responding to the call to write *The Call of the Land*, I also felt the importance of going once more to the land, to live close and to listen. Over the course of my life, I've had the opportunity to contemplate at length in the wilderness over a dozen times, fasting in vision quest with the supervision of experienced elders. Spending stretches of time on the land that way — light and clear, shielded only by a blanket — I felt the land repeatedly convey simple lessons of relationship: "This is mutual. I will take care of you if you respect and take care of me."

Millions of people are listening to the land just now. I regard those who willingly and intelligently respond as 21st Century agrarians. Among them are many experienced and insightful pioneers. Here is a sampling of what they hear.

Greg Bowman is managing editor of *New Farm*, the online magazine of the Rodale Institute in Emmaus, Pennsylvania.

"I was raised on a farm in east Ohio. My dad worked off the farm, but he had a deep passion to be a farmer. Even though he didn't articulate it much, you could see it in him. Living where we did and within fives miles of my grandparents, who had one of the last fully integrated farms in the area with poultry, fruit, vegetables, and all the rest, farms made an early and lasting impression on me. This was before such farms would be called 'multi-phase enterprises.'

"I never saw my grandparents endure the kind of stress that modern people have, what with the banks and marketing and all the rest. I was unaware at the time, and never had the vision to be a farmer, not until I was reporter, assigned by *The*

Salem News in Salem, Ohio to do a weekly farm page. In that job I interviewed a lot of farmers and connected with farmers who want farms to be viable for future generations.

"Then came the first farm crisis of the modern era. The satisfying farm life of people such as my grandparents came to an end because of extreme financial pressures. Farming became much more capital intensive and debt intensive to try and make the farm pay. The farm crisis of the mid-1980s was triggered by a number of macro-economic forces. Plummeting farm values were primary: land and other farm assets declined nearly 50% from their peak in the late 70s to their low point in the mid 80s. Farmers who had invested large sums of money in their farming operations and had high debt loads were hurt the worst because they no longer had the equity to support their loans. Foreclosures and bankruptcies became commonplace as agriculture experienced the biggest shakeout since the Great Depression of the 1930s.

"The social and emotional impacts on farm families were tremendous. Nearly all of the families experienced depression along with a high incidence of withdrawal from family and friends, feelings of worthlessness, mood swings, and increased physical aggressiveness.

"Many people in the community farmed full time and made a good living. They could retire. But by the time I got out of college, that kind of opportunity and experience was more and more rare. It involved so much stress to make the farm pay. The whole way of life was in jeopardy, and the people had a sense of anger and betrayal by the system. They were people who loved to farm and be part of an agrarian community. I identified with this struggle, and wanted to help to tell the story.

"The call I hear from the land now is to a profound reassessment of what sustainability is. To connect in a deep way with the part of society that wants a future. We have an opportunity now in the midst of this current farm crisis. When things quit working — as we see happening now — everything agricultural is open to question. Can farmers use this time to think about what it means to provide food that builds a stronger community?

"If we revert to standard market ideology, and build bigger machines and farm systems, we are in for a difficult time. It's worth the effort to make the obvious and necessary changes. I hope the current farmers and the next generation can find urban and rural networks of support for bioregional food systems, and trade back and forth. Systems that produce food well are going to help solve a lot of problems."

Richard Heinberg is a leading researcher in the field of peak oil and has a long-standing interest in matters agrarian. He is the author of eight books, including *The*

Party's Over and *Powerdown: Options and Actions for a Post-Carbon World*.

"I've been interested in environmental issues for a very long time. It's been the focus of my writing. There are lots of reasons...The latter half of the 20th Century has been one big headlong rush to urbanization and mechanization. I could see the results of this in the impact on environment and also on human psychology. Many people have been increasingly cut off from nature and from any sense of community.

"Lots of people take the mechanization and industrialization of land and food for granted, but for me it was an enormous societal tragedy. I wanted to try to understand why this was happening and to see what could be done about it.

"I am sorry to say that the call of the land I hear right now is a painful gasp. We have been systematically destroying topsoil, ecosystems, species, waterways, and creating dead zones in ocean, you name it. Every biologist I know believes we are in an extinction period right now that rivals and possibly exceeds any in history.

"The land still in many places offers healing and respite from the dreary urban experience with birds, trees, and so on — but it's hard to escape the realization that for most species the ecosystems are being stressed to the breaking point.

"There is a surreal quality to watching all these things unfold. It's one thing to study the trends and to theorize that industrial agriculture is unsustainable, then it's quite another thing to see fertilizer prices skyrocketing, food riots breaking out, the airline industry convulsing, and the auto industry contracting. The reality is that it's alarming and frightening to see it happening, and to see the speed with which it is unfolding."

In addition to the mounting challenges he chronicles, Richard Heinberg sees positive pathways toward the future. He comments on those pathways further on in this book.

Sharon Astyk is co-author, with Aaron Newton, of *A Nation of Farmers: Defeating the Food Crisis on American Soil*. Her focus is on families and what ordinary people can achieve, using ordinary skills and ordinary budgets.

"When I was 20-something, a grad student working on a doctoral dissertation, I was looking around the world. Given what I believe the forthcoming agricultural situation will be, and the current oil situation, I recognized that farms were going to need a lot more people.

"The land requires better stewardship than human beings have given it in a long, long time. Human beings are about to pay the price that they have been deferring.

"Among other things, I have called for a massive return to small-scale agriculture in America as a way of ameliorating the effects of both peak oil and climate change. I argue that doing so would end the disaster of industrial agriculture. It would also help to renew our democracy by reducing our dependence on corporate interests and leading us back towards the Jeffersonian ideal that the US should be a nation of farmers.

"I see two simultaneous trends. More and more large-scale agriculture is the dominant trend around the world. But despite enormous pressure to go that way, we see all over the world — in Latin America, former Soviet Union, and China — a trend toward smaller farms. These trends toward smaller-scale are a response to the need to use our resources wisely.

"I think the larger industrial models are absolutely the wrong way. They are disastrous. Nations like Russia and China that are starting to respond to the need to produce more food, are doing it in intensive plots. They are pointing in the right general direction. Industrial agriculture has, in a sense, taken over the world. But 85 percent of the farms are still small farms. I think we are at the peak of industrial agriculture, and that it will decline from here.

"That's the big trend. The rest of us are going to see — as Cuban agronomists discovered in the 1990s — that large-scale agriculture does not scale well to deal with crisis. We are at the beginning of a large and hotly contested transition to smaller sustainable agriculture. We can go toward it enthusiastically.

"My first book, *Depletion and Abundance: Life on the New Home Front*, was about adapting to a low-energy lifestyle, the idea that we are on a united home front. The last time there was a vast crisis, during World War II, we are called upon to support the war effort at home. We had meatless, and wheatless, and sugarless days, and we are called upon to conserve gas, to narrow the lapels in our clothing, to recycle leftover aluminum pans so the metal could be put to use. All of those things mattered enormously. But then after the war, we were told it didn't matter any more.

"But if it mattered during the crisis of wartime, how you lived and used things, did it stop mattering when the crisis ended? I think not. These are matters of great political importance. We've been sold the idea that these are all private choices, but in fact they are not; they are public choices. When we sit down to eat three times a day it actually has the most consequence in shaping society.

"What does the land require from us if we are to have a future? The biggest and most important challenge is to get the fossil fuels out of agriculture. Fossil fuels are going to come out anyway, whether we want it or not. We have an opportunity to do it wisely now.

"Our present agricultural system depends on heavy inputs of increasingly scarce and expensive fossil fuels. It warms the planet and depletes soil and water and contributes to every major problem we face. But that doesn't have to be the case

— agriculture could help us regenerate our society.

"We need to reclaim our sense of what is important. As long as we vote with our dollars, we can't be empowering things we abhor. It's schizophrenic. We need to empower the land in a way we know is good."

Jerry R. DeWitt is an accomplished photographer and long-time voice for sustainable land use. He serves as director of the Leopold Center for Sustainable Agriculture at Iowa State University (ISU), and coordinates their Extension's Sustainable Agriculture Program. Jerry helped establish an innovative partnership between ISU and the grassroots organization Practical Farmers of Iowa.

"I grew up on a farm, and so impressions were all around me. Then I had an awakening on our land in Iroquois County, Illinois. That was ground zero for Rachel Carson's book *Silent Spring* (1962). The birds had stopped singing. Our farm was in that area, and with observations I began to put it all together.

"What really sparked me on my life path was one of my jobs as a small boy on the farm. My mom would assign tasks by writing them up and putting them in a jar, and then we would pull jobs out of the jar. I often got to 'pick up dead robins off the lawn.' That's because there would always be one or two dead birds per week in our rural setting. I saw the connection between the massive spraying campaign against Japanese beetles in our county, and the dead birds on the lawn. That was a key factor.

"Rachel Carson's book documented the detrimental effects of pesticides on the environment and animals, particularly on birds. I saw the reality of that on our front lawn. Then, my vocation was solidified when we all went through the farm crisis of the mid-1980s, and I was there. I saw the advantage of a smaller-scale farm. At the time I was associate dean in our college of agriculture and extension service. I saw it all. We responded with the resources we had by putting an organic specialist in the field, and we began to move. We knew there needed to be another way, and so we set out to educate about organic, small-scale agriculture being a viable option.

"What I see across the landscape now, not just in Iowa, but across the nation, is an overwhelming feeling of lack of opportunity, of hope and of options. Many farmers feel trapped, and farm families feel there are not too many options left. Not necessarily scared, but they see that their generation may be the last generation on the farm. Mainly because agriculture has now moved to such centralization and specialization, generally, conventional farmers can no longer compete.

"Getting bigger is the only option a lot of farmers see, and that's not too palatable to many of them. Size is not necessarily bad, but the other elements that come with it conspire. Farmers feel trapped because they have lost control of decision making.

Many farmers and ranchers wind up just paying other people to make decisions. When you buy seed, you are also choosing the herbicide and the company to spray, and so forth. It's all linked contractually, and the farmer has no more decisions to make, no choice.

"If you are in agriculture now and want to change, the number one rule is to know that you are probably not going to succeed by trying to compete in the traditional commodity model. Getting bigger won't work for many. Land rent is too damn high. Don't try to compete with the big boys. Start small, maybe 10 or 15 acres. Focus on local, regional marketing, then you will have a distinct advantage. These concepts hold true not just for start-ups, but also for conventional farmers looking for new opportunities.

"The connection is food and agriculture... farmers and ranchers are going to be called upon more to produce grains or meats that are high quality, nutritious, that have qualities the public wants. Consumers see real health concerns and will spend money on it — health is always high on the list. Predictions are that organic products are going to grow."

Leon Secatero — While I was finishing the first draft of this book, my friend Leon Secatero, 65, died (September, 2008). Leon was a true spiritual elder, a gentle leader for the Canoncito Band of I'nabeho (Navajo) of To'Hajiillee, New Mexico, a place on the land about 30 miles west of Albuquerque. He was a bridge builder with a vision, a man with a heartfelt and deeply informed sense of the call of the land. Often and eloquently, Grandfather Leon spoke of what he heard from the land.

"Our 'ancestors' and 'elders' instructions and beliefs are that everything in the world — plants, animals, the land — has a spirit. Everything on the land between the rivers and the mountains is sacred. The natural environment is a critical part of our everyday life. This holistic approach to the world implies that all things in life are related to one another and live according to the universal and natural laws. The elders say we must take care of the land.

"The path and instruction of our ancestors must be initiated because it emphasizes this cooperative and sacred relationship that must exist between people, the environment, the animals, and the plants of Mother Earth.

"It is our responsibility to caretake, in trust for the Creator, all the living things, and to pass from generation to generation the wisdom and knowledge that nurtures the way of life since time immemorial. Traditional awareness perceives the delicate balance existing between all living things with respect and honor for the beauty that Mother Earth has continuously provided us in so many ways. In understanding and acknowledging this we not only fulfill the sacred path, but we also become part of the Mother Earth's beautiful gift.

"The journey we are beginning now is for the next 500 years. What will be the sacred path that people will walk over the next 500 years? Even in the midst of all the changes taking place and all the things falling apart, we are building that foundation now. That's something important for us to remember and to focus on. If we don't do it, no one else will.

"To move ahead into the next 500 years we must leave some things behind or they will contaminate or even eliminate the future. We cannot go forward if we keep destroying the Earth. But we must also ask, what is good and healthy and helpful? Those good things can be part of our foundation, part of our pathway into the next 500 years."

Margaret Krome is policy program director for the Michael Fields Agricultural Institute in East Troy, Wisconsin. The institute's mission is to cultivate the ecological, social, economic, and spiritual vitality of food and farming systems through education, research, and market development. Margaret coordinates the national grassroots campaign to fund federal programs supported by the National Campaign for Sustainable Agriculture.

"After college, I worked as poverty legal aid in Washington, D.C. then I realized I was missing something. Everyone I saw would tell me that I seemed to be missing something, and that I needed to work with the land. It's clear they were right. I have a passion for the land, for forestry, and for how people use, protect and conserve the land.

"I chose the University of Wisconsin-Madison graduate school because of this. There's a strong rural tradition that is so palpable in Wisconsin. This state is an interesting cross section of people and farms. I think I've developed the passion that comes from being around people with passion. I love agricultural issues. I find them thrilling. I love the diversity of opinion around what constitutes good stewardship.

"I think that, among many things, the land is calling out for protection, first of all, from different threats. It's calling out for continued agrarian use in harmony with ecological demands of wildlife, soil and water. I think it is calling out also for systems that do not rob the land in the future to capture gains today. I feel the land calling out for managed grazing systems for livestock, systems that use less fuel, and that keep land covered. They can be more profitable. For new farmers, that creates entry points.

"What's helpful for beginning farmers and ranchers? That manifests itself differently in different parts of country. There are big ethnic differences, and lots of immigrant farmers. A lot of Cambodian and Latino farmers are starting. You'll find them growing in Chicago, Detroit, and southwest Michigan. They operate below the radar. The new farms are multicultural.

"In vegetable production, always a critical part of a system is good crop rotation. If the ground is to be tilled it has to be put into crop rotation. This is old but compelling land knowledge.

"Climate change itself, and the constraints and challenges it imposes, will make a big difference in the future of farming and our food. Crops that used to grow well now find weather too hot or cold or wet or dry for the crops to grow well. You can't plant according to age-old assumptions about the likely weather pattern over the growing season. That makes a big difference in the kind of crops grown. This a huge part of the future understanding of what the land is needing: flexibility and constant awareness from its stewards.

"The ATTRA (National Sustainable Agriculture Information Service) program is a good example of government at its best. They use every penny, squeezing efficiency out of all available funds to respond to people. ATTRA has been around for 20 years, and it's not pork-barrel politics. This is a national service.

"Also, the SARE (Sustainable Agriculture, Research, and Education) program is wonderful. They are totally responsive to what farmers and ranchers need. Over the years they have developed a lot of good programs."

Shoshanah Inwood was co-founder of Silver Tale Organic Farm in northeastern Ohio in 2000, and served on the board of the Ohio Ecological Food and Farm Association while studying for a Ph.D. in Rural Sociology at Ohio State University. In 2008 the USDA's Sustainable Agriculture and Research (SARE) program sponsored a New Voices contest. Shoshanah emerged as the winner for her presentation, *Advancing the Frontier of Sustainable Agriculture in the coming 20 Years: A Roadmap to the Future*.

"I ... believe that the way a country feeds itself speaks to our values, humanity, and the legacy we leave the next generation. We move forward when we build an agriculture rooted in our shared values of family, community, health, and prosperity.

"I did not grow up on farm, but when I was finishing up college, my senior year in the late '90s studying biology and botany at Oberlin, I began to look more closely. After graduation I did a conservation internship at Malabar State Park, and began to ponder: what are the issues? What are we doing with land beyond the short-term?

"What I hear from the land is that it's time to put away the distractions. Don't waste time dickering over definitions of sustainability or organic, but how as a society, as a community will we work our land. We can't afford to play games. We must work ecologically. No single production method is the answer. We need all different sizes and skills. The land has many environmental niches, so we need to respond to particulars. It's a complex story.

"In an era of climate change and energy uncertainty, it has become ever more urgent that we build ecologically based agricultural systems that promote healthy water and soil systems on our farms and thriving rural communities.

"But how do we do this? Technical solutions give us only part of the answer. To create fundamental change we must build new bridges in the farming community, find strength in the diversity of American farmers and consumers and use food as a platform for expanding farm policy debates. Only then can we ensure the widespread adoptions necessary for true change.

"A lesson we learn from ecology is the strength diversity can lend to biological and social systems. When fields and communities include a wide range of crops, farm sizes and types—and our organizations embrace an array of voices—we become stronger, more resilient and better able to adapt to a changing world. The building blocks for a new agriculture are the country's 'New American Farmers,' who represent diverse perspectives from multi-generation, first generation, women, minority, immigrant and limited resource farmers.

"One answer is to expand farmer mentoring programs. Younger farmers would live and work with a skilled farmer-mentor who would guide them through production and accounting practices. These experiences should include the whole farm family so that parents, spouses and children feel a part of the process.

"Food is part of our social foundation, and a potent mechanism for connecting producers, eaters, and decision makers. Food is a springboard for addressing a host of issues facing the country: land use policy, the rural-urban interface, environmental regulation, trade agreements, and alternative energy—to name just a few."

Trauger Groh has farmed the land in Germany and the United States throughout his life. At age 76, he is somewhat retired, though he still grazes 10 heifers and feeds the sheep through the winters at the Temple-Wilton Community Farm in New Hampshire, a farm he helped found, and one of the first two CSA farms established in America. I had the honor of working with him in the 1990s as we co-authored *Farms of Tomorrow*, and its sequel seven years later, *Farms of Tomorrow Revisited*.

"I have listened to the land for a very long time," Trauger told me. "When I was young and living in Germany, I lost my family farm to the military for an airfield. Then I had to decide, do I want to stay in farming? Yes, but never on a traditional family farm. I could see the reality of it. My neighbors were completely stressed all the time trying to make ends meet. I did not want to go in that direction. That is why we started something called community farms (CSAs).

"What we tried here, and what I feel more and more people will want in the future, is a group of independent farms in associative relationship. For farming you need independent people. Why? You see, if you work in nature with animals or feed crops, you have to take a deep personal interest in it. The hired person cannot do this. A salary is insufficient motivation. You need a deep personal interest in caring for the land and animals. We need another way. The land is crying, calling for human hands.

"We have no employees on our farm here. We have partners. At the Temple-Wilton Community Farm our principle has been to run the farm by a group of independent farmers in association with each other, not employees. Employment is the last outgrowth of slavery. If you are employed, you have to work on order. The employer sets the tone and says what you must do. People won't want that in the future.

"The land needs more people to take an interest. That means we need many more farmers in the future, which will come anyway because the oil is peaking. Industrial farming is built on oil — so we will need many, many new farmers.

"The farms of today, devoted to either livestock or field crops, will not lead us into the future. We need both. We need animals, and better rotation with grasses and clover. How that will come about one does not know. But the scarcity and price of oil in the future will drive this. A farm's economy should be based on cover crops — grass, alfalfa, clover, and this needs animals to produce manure. Today we concentrate the animals on big feed lots, then manure becomes an environmental problem. But used on farms in the proper way, manures will keep fertility up.

"One could have a healthy agriculture even on big farms, but one has to bring animals back to the farm, and have green crops in the rotation, to keep up and to develop soil fertility. Even in the monoculture of corn and soy in the Midwest, things will need to change. We need a better rotation. We have to build up the soils again, and can do this only with grass, clover, alfalfa.

"The land requires that we embrace a more spiritual understanding of nature. You cannot do farming just as a business. It is the basis of life on Earth for humankind. If we do agriculture with our primary focus on it as a business, we end up in a disaster fertility wise, and also food quality wise. That is why I was long ago called to biodynamic farming, because it has a an understanding of the spiritual dimension of nature."

Brad Masi is Executive Director of the New Agrarian Center in Cleveland, Ohio. The center is committed to building a stronger, more sustainable regional food system in Northeast Ohio.

"In our workaday lives we easily spend the majority of our time in artificial, manufactured environments. Our buildings, our food, our methods of communication — most of these take us away from any sense of connection to the land and the natural world. Yet, as ecologist Paul Sears wrote back in 1930, our bodies are on loan to us from the Earth. Everything that we need to function daily comes from the Earth. Whether we consciously acknowledge it or not, we are always tied to the Earth.

"What called me to the land is a profound sense of the elegance of natural systems, and a need to feel a visceral connection to the Earth. When I eat a meal, I want to know the soil, people, and watershed that nurtured the meal. I want to know that natural systems are intact and actually enhanced by the meal. If my meal degrades soils, people, or forests, then I am forsaking the future and not replacing what has been consumed.

"The most encouraging work that I have been involved with over the past few years is the application of agrarianism to urban areas. I worked with several other community partners to initiate City Fresh, a social enterprise that seeks to improve food access in inner-city neighborhoods.

"Cleveland has been particularly hard-hit by the equivalent of a sustained, slow-motion hurricane that has seen a steady erosion of the local economy since the 1950s. The foreclosure crisis hit Cleveland hard. The community fabric that once held so many neighborhoods together has been torn. Yet I see food as one of the gathering points for rebuilding a sense of community and connection to nature in a harsh, rust-belt environment.

"I recall hearing a city councilman in a particularly hard-hit ward of Cleveland describing a French film crew that came out to film a documentary on the foreclosure crisis in America. He was struck by how fixated the film crew became on a group of people working in a neighborhood garden. In the midst of all these boarded-up houses and empty storefronts, people were engaged in a hopeful activity — working together to grow food in a small patch of urban decay.

"There is a growing agrarian movement in many of the traditional rust-belt cities of the Great Lakes as people and community connect to clean up and reclaim vacant lots. As the agrarian values of thrift, community, land stewardship, and local economy take hold in cities like Cleveland, we can see the building blocks for a regenerative economy start to emerge. What better place to engage in this work than the place that propelled national concern about our environmental plight with a river that actually caught on fire and burned?"

Steve Diver worked for ATTRA (National Sustainable Agriculture Information Service) for 18 years in Fayetteville, Arkansas. He now works with Sustainable Growth

Texas, a private company that offers consultations and sells biology-based materials for soil fertility.

"My own connection with the land arose as a young boy when I first joined the Boy Scouts. We lived in Tulsa, and we went on campouts in eastern Oklahoma, in the foothills of the Ozarks, and we encountered mosses, lichens, trees, and rocks. I found it all fascinating. Having that experience, then later in high school when I worked part time in a retail garden center, really did it for me. I knew I was going into horticulture and botany.

"Then I got to college at Oklahoma State University in Stillwater in the mid-1970s. The first or second year a group of us went in and created a huge community garden in someone's backyard. Parts of it were just a smash hit. At the same time some of the other stuff just struggled. That observation got me to thinking: 'There's got to be a better way to do this. There's old timers around who can probably explain this.'

"Where does farming and gardening wisdom come from? My career took off with those questions, and that's how I've approached consulting ever since. I read extension bulletins and research reports, and I talk with people who have real experience. My specialty is helping farmers grow healthy food.

"In the history of agriculture one thing that stands out in people's minds is the Green Revolution, which is synonymous with modern agriculture and chemical-based fertilizers, pesticides, and hybrid seeds. That's pretty much the norm these days: chemical-based inputs. But now we are at the turning point where, instead of alternative-minded farmers making inquiries about the best ways to grow food cleanly, you have a large segment of American farmers who are inquiring. At work we are seeing an increase in inquiries from all kinds of farmers as the price of fertilizer skyrockets. They want to know: 'How do I raise my crops without chemical fertilizer?'

"When I was with ATTRA, one of the things we would discuss with farmers, to help them grasp sustainability was to say, 'Imagine a time when the costs of nitrogen fertilizers are so expensive that you are looking for alternatives like legumes and compost?' Well that imaginary scenario is here.

"Remember that in general any piece of land in nature is receptive. Any degraded land that you encounter and engage can be remediated — brought back to healthy life with the proper principles and practices that mimic nature. If you manage the soil and take care of it, then you are promoting the basic life-giving cycle that wants to come forth. All kinds of land can be brought back.

"One of the biggest, most successful things to happen in the modern era of US history is market farming and the CSA (Community Supported Agriculture) movement. Their development has been simultaneous. The equipment and techniques that came out of organic farming are the base for that. That's been huge.

"Smaller-scale is always easier to work with than larger tracts of land. I work with farmers and gardeners who are ready and willing, open to make changes. There are lots of opportunities. We have the technologies. It's people we need. When people are ready to implement these changes then it works out well. There's the equipment, the tools, and the techniques of market farming with lots of options on philosophy. It's gotten sophisticated. These approaches have blossomed over the last 15 years. All this is available to people right now, right at a time when we need it."

Courtney White is executive director of The Quivira Coalition in Santa Fe, New Mexico, and author of *Revolution on the Range: The Rise of a New Ranch in the American West*.

When I interviewed Courtney for this book, he began our conversation by asking if I knew the word *querencia*. It is both a Spanish-language word and a metaphysical concept. It describes a place where one feels safe, a place from which one's strength of character is drawn, a place where one feels at home. In bullfighting, the bullfighter prepares for the kill that will end it. But a bull may stake out turf — querencia — a place in the ring where he feels strong and safe, even when surrounded by a strong wooden fence and a looming assemblage of human beings who have gathered to behold the spectacle. As Courtney sees it, querencia is something we are needing to create for ourselves now via our farms, ranches, and public lands.

"I grew up in the Sonoran Desert in Arizona. I spent many years walking the land as a boy, and then later as an archaeologist. It got into my system at a young age. The land became all, although I didn't think of it that way at the time. I had a strong sense of land also from horseback, as I rode. My family was not ranchers, but my parents both came from ranch families. They were not agrarians, but they loved the land, and from them I learned how to be outdoors and how to camp.

"At age 15 I set off on a backpack odyssey in the National Parks. I saw the wide world, and how many different places there are here in America, and I heard the call of the public land — the land we own together. As an adult, even though my degree was in anthropology, I took work as an archaeologist. Through that I came to see the land in other ways, and to have a different relationship as I sorted through the remains of other older cultures and reflected on how they had lived. Being outdoors, and seeing so closely the human impact, I took a strong impression.

"When I listen now the land is telling me that it is in poor condition across the West. That's plain to anyone who looks carefully. So the question is, what do we do to heal it?

"The traditional response of environmentalists has been to isolate the endangered land, and leave it alone in hopes that it would recover. But now human impact is everywhere. There's no escaping what is going on all over our planet. So we must face it. The oldest task in human history is finding a way to live successfully off a piece of land. We have to figure that out now together, and the piece of land is our Earth. We all depend on it, and we all have to ensure that it is healthy and productive.

"Through the Quivira Coalition we do not involve ourselves in politics or legislation, we are simply an alliance of ranchers and environmentalists. Our questions are, 'How do we get our land into better shape? How do we put a new agrarian movement together?' I think the future lies at the nexus of ecology and agriculture.

"Our attention and energy needs to be focused now on ecology and agriculture. The new agrarianism can't be just about food or small farms or small ranches. It needs to be about land and local energy. They go together. You have got to have local energy to enable you to be on the land sustainably. We need a new movement, a fusion of agrarians, conservationists, and land-health scientists. There is a great need for fusion across tribal boundaries."

Denise O'Brien is co-founder of Women, Food & Agriculture Network, a national and international alliance to support and amplify women's voices on critical matters of rural, agricultural, and environmental systems.

"I did not grow up on a farm, but I believe there was something of the land always within me. Part of it was that my family always had a garden and so I picked peas and lettuce and so forth, and saw that my dad was a hunter and fisher to provide for our family. Until my father had some sons, I filled the companion role: I'd go squirrel hunting with dad, learned to handle a gun, and went fishing in muddy rivers in Western Iowa. I always liked it, going out early in the morning, sitting on riverbanks and waiting for bullheads and catfish.

"When hunting with my dad I walked across the land, and it somehow transferred to me respect for Mother Nature and all the creatures. There's lots of things about my dad. He was a stickler who made his sons carry their guns for a year before they got to shoot. So definitely that's where I learned that.

"When I moved from home as a rotary club student, I lived in four different households, before coming back home to Iowa in 1975, back to the small town where I grew up. My mom was very ill, and I wanted to stay with her and get reacquainted with Iowa.

"A month later I met a man. He'd been traveling around the nation, and he wanted to farm organically. Within six months we were married, and so I began my farming career. That really planted me here. I think it's incredible that I met a farmer, that I fell in love with my husband, Larry. Now, as we mark 32 years of marriage, we celebrate the things we believe in, which have become realities.

"In those days when Larry and I were starting out there was no place to learn about organic agriculture, but I did read the publications coming out of Rodale. The Cornucopia Project of the Rodale Institute in the early 1980s was the beginning of our study about local food. We started buying clubs, and so forth, and learned about regional food sufficiency. The things we learned outside of where we live, we brought back here and so over time we became examples and leaders. You know that old saying, 'we are the ones we have been waiting for.'

"In 2006 I ran for Secretary of Agriculture in Iowa, which is an elected position here. I told my husband I really don't want to sing to the choir anymore, but to reach out. Traveling through the state during the campaign I saw the projects going on in agriculture in every county. There are so many promising projects. I talked with people in audiences about local food, food in schools. I got to visit lots of sites, little projects all over, with a small group. It occurred to me during that time that when things fall apart, it will be these kinds of places that people turn to for leadership...

"I ran for Secretary of Agriculture as an organic farmer, but I lost and so went on to other opportunities. The most attention I pay now is to the acres we farm. We have pared down to 16 acres in asparagus, berries, and apples. My attention is here, the living voice is where our land is, an organic, diversified base, not a commodity farm. But the land all around us is being pillaged for biofuels. Everything has a voice, and maybe I don't want to hear that industrial agricultural voice, because it is overwhelmingly troubled.

"Still, I am optimistic about the future. I see so many incredibly intelligent youth who are strongly interested in agriculture, even though they don't necessarily come from farms. These young people have a real healthy attachment to the land, and you can see this trend growing in urban, suburban, and rural areas.

"I traveled to Carleton College in Minnesota for a Women, Food and Politics conference, and got to spend time with many wonderful women interested in going back to the land. I've seen this a lot over the last 10 years. Young women come to me and express their desire to be on the land farming. It's noteworthy that women are entering farming as men are leaving. They are entering on a small scale, and often with livestock as part of the farm. That's a wise choice.

"What I see about them, and I might be living in a bubble exposed to the best and brightest, but these small, liberal arts colleges are very pertinent to the change that is happening for the future, especially the environmental classes. Intellectually the students find out about it, and immediately understand how broadly the Earth is endangered. Then they come to the land."

John Kimmey is a seed planter with the scope of a visionary and the skill set of a community developer. In the 1970s he became acquainted with the traditional Hopi elders at Hotevilla, Arizona. At their request, he settled in to assist them in communicating with the United Nations and various national governments. He became a student and traveling companion of the late Hopi messenger and village leader, David Monongye.

"When I associated with Native American elders, they encouraged me to grow gardens. Grandfather David gave me blue corn seeds and asked me to grow them out. He said 'I want you to experiment. The first experiment is to divide the seeds, then to grow two separate plots: one right next to where you are camped, the other further away, out of earshot.'

"I planted both plots of corn on the same day, and did normal irrigation and cultivation with both. Grandfather told me to sing to just one of the plots, the one closest to where I slept. I awoke each morning at dawn and sang to the crop nearest, and I also sang whenever I cultivated. I asked what song I should sing, and Grandfather said to sing any song that is meaningful to me, and to sing every day.

"As it turned out at harvest time, the sung corn matured a week earlier than the control corn, with more ears per stalk, and the ears had transformed from the more typical dull blue to a rich, vibrant purple color. I went back and gave Grandfather David the results, and he nodded with understanding. He said the ancestors always sang to their crops, especially during drought. 'Song makes them stronger,' he said.

"Grandfather said that your cultivars — the seeds you save and grow — become part of your family. 'Treat them with the same love, care, and attention that you show to your children.'

"What I hear from the land now is a theme of 'resolution.' We have through split consciousness created severe polarities, and they are constantly trying to resolve themselves to balance. Our consciousness is the key to resolution. When we resolve ourselves, the land does, too.

"Begin your relationship with nature and farming on a personal level, grow your own backyard garden, no matter what else you do. The garden will serve as your mentor. Any questions you may have you can answer through your own experiments in the garden. From that you can begin to achieve a relationship with the land and the plants and the climate. That will be your source of guidance in the future. You can consider that as your main teacher."

Ben Gisin began his career working for banks as a specialist in agricultural credit. After 20 years, culminating as the senior approval officer for the nation's seventh largest agricultural bank, and publishing the book *Farmers and Ranchers Guide to Credit*, he left banking to start a new career.

"When I left banking in 1996, I began offering consulting services to farmers and ranchers who face credit challenges. What I surmised to be a practice of coaching and helping farmers put together credit applications turned out to be a practice that put me in the middle of forces that are economically unsustainable: farmers fighting for money and lenders fighting to get the money. Ultimately, I spent most of my time negotiating many large and difficult debt settlements between farm lenders and farm borrowers.

"Having been involved in the financial affairs of thousands of farming enterprises, approving billions of dollars of credit extensions, visiting an untold number of farms and fighting on behalf of a beleaguered rural America, I found it to be obvious that the nation's food production in terms of economics, mainstream cultural practices and land and water availability was not only unsustainable, but increasing in its scope of unsustainability.

"Because agriculture is the single largest physical event on our planet — directly impacting 38 percent of land — two things need to be born: a new agricultural system and a new financial system. They are both so huge that we can't ignore them. If everyone is going to eat, we're going to have to make changes in both arenas. So in 2005, with Susan Gisin as editor, we launched our publication, *Touch the Soil* with a mission to cover broad topics such as agricultural awareness for both urban and farming people on issues like farmland, water, global food crises, food security, food safety, global and national food and farming issues. Our aim is to report on the best ideas, people and practices, and to explore the economic sustainability of food production within the larger financial system.

"When we first started, we felt a global food crisis was coming. We thought we'd put food security as our focus: food safety, availability, economics of acquiring food, and so forth. We thought, we really need to be geared toward consumers to raise agricultural awareness, to let them to know that there is a simpler, cleaner way. We have paved enough of the planet that we can't have all of our food from local sources. But we can have a lot more.

"In people's minds they think of money as our means of exchange, but really money doesn't exist. If we walk into a bank and ask to borrow money, it's all a false concept. The bank does not have money. First you sign an agreement on collateral.

The bank now has an asset. The bank then puts a number on your bank account statement. So when you get your balance statement, it shows assets and liabilities, but no money. Checking accounts are merely the liabilities of a bank. But if you write a check to a friend, you are not really transferring money; in practicality, what your bank owes you is now transferred over to what your friend's bank owes him. It's accounting wizardry. But it has important applications in today's economy.

"Industrial agriculture and our general culture are very much a reflection of the way we interact. The goal of industrial agriculture is to make money. When you are competing for money, it cultivates the lowest human mentality — cutting corners on quality, and environment, and social factors be damned.

"But in the bigger picture of agriculture, loans or credits are never a substitute for income. In our current economic system there are exceptions to those rules, yet in the bigger picture, our mechanism of exchange is based on obligations. I become obligated to the bank, the bank becomes obligated to me. But what about now when we are up to trillions of dollars in bank obligations?

"There's not a simple answer for this reason: the financial system products — deposits and currency — require that the economy take on ever increasing levels of debt. So the economy becomes increasingly saturated with debt — everything: individuals, families, communities, business, and governments are all saturated with debt. First thing that people do is say Pay bills, Eat, Keep a roof over your head? This is a mathematical absurdity that grinds us down.

"Over the years I've seen so many farmers lose 30 to 40 percent of a season's potential production because they were waiting for loans, waiting to be saddled with debt. At a fundamental level, that's not right. The human family is going to have to come up with other methods of exchange. But possibilities are emerging."

By way of example, Ben told me that one of the largest "grocery stores" is food banking. It is a food distribution system that operates through the help of over a million volunteers who work through a wide network of non-profit, tax-exempt organizations. Via these food banks, he said, the human family is learning that in the future cooperation and volunteerism may be playing a larger role in our economy. We may have to cooperate rather than compete.

"There are quite a few barter exchanges, places online like barternews.com, where several hundred businesses come to share information about their products and services, and where a lot of activity takes place without the need for cash. It's a network of fair exchange.

"I think that the economy, to sustain moving forward, needs to look at the models of those businesses and individuals that can think outside the box. Wherever they can, they get other economic compensation beyond money. We need to focus on that basic exchange concept. Because the financial system is less and less able to get money to show up at the right time in the right place, work for food will be becoming more and more predominant. We've still got to find ways to get food from field to plate."

James Harrison — "Ever since I was a little kid I always loved the land. I used to play and build little civilizations in our backyard in Lincoln, Massachusetts. As I got older I had opportunities to work on farms. I made hay at Codman Farm, and often visited my cousins who lived on what were called gentleman farms. Then when I went to college at Macalester in St. Paul, Minnesota, I got more interested in geography and land use. Eventually, I just kind of paired up my physical work with a more philosophical piece having to do with the land. I felt that if I were farming and doing something productive on the land, then I could be sure of something: that one plot of the Earth was being taken care of well.

"Then The Food Project started in in 1991 in Lincoln. I was interested, but already too old to participate. So when I came home to visit my parents, I would volunteer to help out with little projects. Through that I came to realize I want to be here closer to my parents, and also to be a part of The Food Project as it expanded.

"The call of the land hasn't changed much. It can be hard to listen beyond the farm's task list for the day, but one thing I often see is that the world is changing so fast. But then you go back to the farm and it feels the same as always. There's a very primal thing there. People have been growing these kinds of crops for thousands of years, with some technical improvements, but in some ways it feels the same as it did a thousand years ago.

"One of the things I love about farming is the Emersonian concept of pitting your own ideas about the way nature works against what really goes on in the world. It's very satisfying to try to understand what's going on in the natural world, and then to take intelligent action based on that. When it works out it is so cathartic. To me it feels good, that constant observation of what's going on and then coming up with the best response.

"I had been the head grower on our farm in Beverly, but I'm now director of agriculture for The Food Project, so I oversee all farming activity. Still, I'm out on the land a couple of hours a day. The new position was created because the farm staff is already so busy, working on the tasks at hand, that we recognized that to successfully expand farming operations and progress, somebody had to be looking around and not just buried in the chores and challenges at hand.

"One of the things The Food Project is doing that's innovative and exciting is the

Build a Garden project. We got funding to build 100 raised-bed gardens in Boston's neighborhoods of Dorchester, Mattapan, and Roxbury. We come in with a van of soil and farmers and create the raised beds, and teach classes to new gardeners. I see an exploding interest in community gardens and backyard gardens. That has a practical economic side, arising out of a concern about food availability."

Woody Wodraska and Barbara Scott have been partners on the land for many years, farming many places on the Earth, including British Columbia, Idaho, Virginia, and New Hampshire. They now write and consult on agrarian matters, including farming and composting.

Woody is the author of *Deep Gardening: Soul Lessons from 17 Gardens*. "I have written from time to time about how we will all be gardeners in the future. This is the way it was a couple of hundred years ago and further back for ten thousand years. I don't mean every one of us will be a gardener. There have always been classes of people who ordered the others about, or interceded with the gods, or made a living by trading, but I feel that in the future by far the majority of us will be close to the Earth and living out its rhythms.

"It's only been people of the past few generations who have lived in a culture that has forced their estrangement from the land, with the authorities-that-be, the prevailing economic and political pooh-bahs, always abstracting themselves one step further away from the realities of seasons and harvests. What will redeem us is real food grown in real soil by real individuals manifesting real intent."

In independent interviews, both Woody and Barbara cited Rudolf Steiner, the initiator of biodynamic agriculture. "Nutrition as it is today does not supply the strength necessary for manifesting the spirit in physical life," Steiner wrote. "A bridge can no longer be built from thinking to will and action. Food plants no longer contain the forces people need for this."

Barbara told me, "I hear from Mother Earth that the time is now for small farms and other land holders to get with levity. When I say 'levity' I mean education that is light-filled, that arises from the wisdom of direct experience. The 'classroom' is the Earth. She is our teacher.

"By levity I mean rising to a new vibration that is light — not too heavy, even though it is serious. The future will be better than imagined. We have a tendency to go in our minds to the notions that it's all doom and gloom as we hear the news. But if we do that to ourselves, the doom and gloom also goes out into the fields we live on. If we put something new and light into our thoughts and dreams, it will be broadcast to the fields as well.

"This is the time we live in. It could be a curse to be born in an age of crisis, but only if we do not also realize that there are great opportunities, perhaps the biggest opportunities ever. We are it. We have to act as the transition team. We are like halfbacks; the young ones will deliver the touchdowns.

"We are in the middle of preparing the ground. I've had a chance to travel and teach in Africa, and I was impressed by an old African proverb. 'Blessed are the young ones who have so far to go; blessed are the elders who have come so far; and blessed are those in the middle who are doing the work.'

"We need to establish an economy based on the needs of the land as opposed to what the markets are demanding, and to begin building up a teaching archive for all, especially for farmers and gardeners, where the motivating force is that of working the Earth in accordance with Spirit, thereby making a beginning towards paying off the spiritual debt we owe her. And restoring the quality of life on our planet.

"Farmers can no longer focus solely on making a living, rather than focusing on the needs of the land. The times they are a changing. We have to first be guardians and caretakers of the land if she is ever going to take care of us. Our planet is in peril. The concept 'Think globally, act locally' is still valid."

Barbara and Woody are both influenced by Manfred Klett, a farmer and philosopher who pointed out that if people, and society, go through a historical phase without a plan, it can easily turn into evil. "That's how he talks about nuclear power, radiation, hormones, genetically engineered plants, industrialized anything," Barbara said. "Many of these things have come into being without a conscious plan and have gone awry, causing significant problems...What is our plan for the land now? Does anybody have a plan? Here's my plan: nourish, encourage, and catalyze for the future."

Chapter Two
Agrarian Ethos

"There is another way to live and think: it's called agrarianism. It is not so much a philosophy as a practice, an attitude, a loyalty and a passion—all based in close connection with the land. It results in a sound local economy in which producers and consumers are neighbors and in which nature herself becomes the standard for work and production." ~ Wendell Berry ~

The basic equation is direct. Our food arises from agriculture, which arises from the land, which is essential to our survival. When this web of life is threatened—as it is now—we are in direct peril. As a consequence at this opening phase of the 21st Century, we require *metanoia* — the term from classical Greek for a fundamental shift in the way we understand and live in the world.

Rachel Carson, author of the landmark book *Silent Spring*, made the key point long ago: "Man's attitude toward nature is today critically important simply because we now have acquired a fateful power to alter and destroy nature. But man is part of nature, and his war is inevitably a war against himself."

Now is the time to apply our strength, intelligence, and will to making peace with the land that is the basis of our survival. The genesis of this peace lies in the realm of our ethos.

The word *ethos* originates from the Greek root *ethikos*, meaning moral, and is the root of our modern English-language term for moral competence: ethics. Ethos arises out of communal experience and insight, and denotes a people's characteristic spirit — their guiding beliefs and values.

As we confront radically changing circumstances in our economy, energy supply, and food chain, we have an opportunity to change and reconstitute our agrarian ethos and the way we live with the land. We can make a deliberate shift not just out of necessity, but also out of wisdom.

In his book, *A Sand County Almanac,* Aldo Leopold asserted that nothing as important as a land ethic could ever be written. It must instead, he said, exist in the minds and hearts of the people as an authentic product of their social evolution. "All ethics so far evolved rest upon a single premise: that the individual is a member of a community of interdependent parts. His instincts prompt him to compete for his place in that community, but his ethics prompt him also to cooperate (perhaps in order that there may be a place to compete for)."

Leopold has a valid point in observing that, to be real, an ethos must be the living experience of the people, not a written theory. But we also need continued writing, discussion, and debate about our land, for these activities create opportunities for an illumined ethos to take root in our souls.

None of us can survive if we do not respect the land as an integral part of our modern culture. A new agrarianism for the 21st Century can guide us to do just that. By embracing and evolving an agrarian ethic in response to the stark planetary facts of our era, and consequently changing the way we cultivate our land, we can establish a base of renewal for our whole culture.

We have the possibility of manifesting a solid, agrarian foundation that is rooted in experience, adapted to the specific, contemporary needs of our Earth, oriented to the future for the next seven generations of our children, and capable of integrating high-tech, sustainable energy, tools, and practices.

We already are the beneficiaries of a great number of positive agrarian developments. Sustainable initiatives have been coming forward for over 60 years, building steadily on the agrarian traditions of earlier centuries. By now there exists a host of workable models that individuals, communities, corporations, and networks can learn from and emulate.

Three elements arise frequently in the many definitions of sustainable agriculture: environmentally sound, economically viable, and socially fair. This is a concise expression of the emerging agrarian ethos.

In 2006 a total of 96 nations sent delegations to Brazil for the International Conference on Agrarian Reform and Rural Development. They issued a joint declaration acknowledging the essential role of agrarian reform and rural development to promote sustainable development of the planet.

They reaffirmed that "wider, secure and sustainable access to land, water and other natural resources" on which rural people depend is "essential to hunger and poverty eradication, which contribute to sustainable development."

More and more, studies are showing that organic agriculture can in fact feed the world, and that, rather than creating environmental problems, organic agriculture heals and enlivens the land.

Because organic farming maintains a natural and healthy diversity of the ecosystem, it creates safe havens for pollinating bees, birds, and bats, which are absolutely necessary for planetary life, and which are now threatened with global systemic extinction.

An increasingly large number of studies shows organic food is healthier than chemicalized, industrially processed food. Organic food contains more nutrients and vitamins and minerals, and is clear of pesticide and herbicide residues.

Because it doesn't contain expensive chemical inputs and reduces the use of medicines in animal husbandry, organic farming can be a less-expensive method of food production. Organic farming helps reduce global climate change because its methods use animal manure and cover crops like clover and legumes to enrich the soil which also helps sequester CO_2 from the atmosphere.

All this was acknowledged by The United Nations Food and Agricultural Organization (FAO) in 2008, when they published a report stating that a system of organic agriculture combining indigenous knowledge and modern science could address local and global food security challenges. The report asserted that a worldwide shift to organic agriculture will fight world hunger and at the same time help reduce climate change.

When I co-authored *Farms of Tomorrow* with Trauger Groh, we articulated three basic motivations for farming. This expression of motivations bears repeating to establish a context for the ethical statements that follow:

- To help create life anew every year so human beings can be born safely and have healthy bodies that allow them to live out their destinies.
- To provide adequate food, wood, and fiber for people, so no one will be forced to live without.
- To steward the Earth in such a way that it brings forth an abundance of clean food and water for this and following generations, and by so doing to propagate beauty that uplifts the human soul.

Ethical Statements

The following statements arise not so much from my original thoughts, but as a journalist's effort to synthesize the observations of many insightful farmers, writers, and thinkers. In that sense, I am striving to accurately echo our collective folk wisdom, as I hear it, in the early part of this new millennium. Generations of farmers and researchers have gained this knowledge. My task is to compile this wisdom and offer it as a reminder of agrarian fundamentals that may serve us and our land through the 21st Century. I offer these ethical statements not as dogma, but in an effort to clarify thought and stimulate further engagement.

Animals — Animals are our relatives, and they sustain us through their lives and the sacrifice of their deaths that we may have meat for our tables. For common-sense purposes as well as basic respect for life, animals merit our compassionate care and attention. We must find new, humane ways of tending our herds and flocks that we may have meat — ways that don't imprison animals in vast, crowded, reeking cages and feedlots, or subject them to mass chemical exploitation and genetic experiments.

Historically, manure from farm animals was a form of gold. Today, farms without livestock fight an uphill battle for fertility. When massed on huge, confined feedlots and barns, animals produce a volume and quality of manure that has become an enormous environmental problem. But when animals are raised on a common-sense scale and given access to the natural world, then their manure can become a primary source of vitality and fertility.

Ruminants are the ultimate solar energy converters. Their manure from the field is nature's ideal fertilizer when gathered, wisely composted, and spread back onto the land. With factory farmed animals we don't get manure; we get titanic pools of toxic waste that create ongoing environmental problems.

Draft horses, mules and oxen are beautiful, powerful creatures. Breeding them in large numbers to serve moderate-scale farms has many benefits.

Consumers — Every dollar we spend is a direct vote for how the land is treated, and the kind of agrarian ethos we endorse. We are wise to invest carefully, based on knowledge. The market is where people purchase food, learn about its origin, interact with community members and meet the farmers who grow their food. This is a vital arena for the expression of an agrarian ethos.

Diversity — Diversified farms that grow a wide variety of crops and serve as home to animal herds are usually small enough so the farmer gains an intimate and beneficial knowledge of the land. Producing a variety of crops leads to improved farm profitability, water quality, fish health, carbon sequestration, and decreased greenhouse gas emissions and soil erosion.

Racial, ethnic, and religious diversity is a fact of life. The grace that arises from accepting this reality establishes a certain quality mirrored in the grace of a diversified farm.

Economy — The prevailing assumption of the marketplace is that higher, more-profitable production is always better. But how shall we define profit? Is it just for now, for this year, or does it extend into next year, or even to the years when our children and grandchildren will walk the land? Is monetary profit based on something real, or is it a series of symbolic blips on a computer screen?

Capitalist economics puts profit at the heart of all enterprises. Communist economics puts the state at the heart of all enterprises. But there are other paths. Associative economy, for example, holds that we must put the needs of human beings at the heart of our economic activity, and recognize that true wealth comes not from credit schemes, but from the land.

The concept of associative economy was first expounded by Austrian philosopher Rudolf Steiner at the start of the 20th Century, and has slowly been developed in theory and practice by others in the following decades. This concept — consciously or unconsciously — underlies many community-supported farms (CSAs).

The basic idea of associative economics is to identify the true needs in a given situation, and then to cover those needs with the least effort (least input of energy, labor, and substances). Associative economy posits that all the participants in a given economic process — such as a CSA farm — strive to listen to the needs of all other partners in the process. Active farmers listen to the needs of the member households; member households listen to the needs of the farmers. All attune themselves to the needs of the land, so it will yield bounty in an ongoing, sustainable, and clean manner. On this basis, the farm proceeds. No one asks, "How can we make more money?" Profit isn't the motive with associative economy. The questions are, instead, "What do the land, the active farmers, and the member families actually need? How can we meet those needs together?"

Environmental Commons — The evolving concept of an environmental commons recognizes that we all have a common stake in the air, water and soil. We work together to defend our environmental heritage: water, air, biodiversity, and genetic variability. As our "commons," they are directly linked to the quality of our lives. We must live and work with shared understanding to preserve our natural areas, protect wildlife, and promote clean, sustainable use of the land.

Forces — Healthy plants and animals develop between heaven and Earth, becoming an expression of both substances and forces. Thus, agriculture is not a strictly materialistic enterprise. In addition to the physical substance of the land that supports our crops and herds, we must reckon with forces, or energies long personified in folk cultures around the world through Earth, air, fire, water, and ether: gnomes, sylphs, fairies, angels, little people, and Leprechauns. Recognition of these forces is deeply rooted in the human soul, as evidenced by their universal nature. On that basis alone, they merit consideration. Whether they're cultural icons or defined in scientific terms, these forces play an equal role with the material substances of a farm or a garden.

Foundation — Agriculture is the base upon which modern civilization rests. Without a steady supply of clean, life-giving food, we have neither the leisure nor the energy to develop industry, science, or art. Food is a basic human need. Every person must eat. This was acknowledged as a global ethical principle in 1996 by the Food and Agriculture Organization of the UN: "Every man, woman and child has the right to be free from hunger and malnutrition."

Health — Agrarians realize food is intended to be clean and to nourish, giving strength, health, and clarity of mind. Food should not infest the body with microtraces of synthetic, petroleum-based pro-inflammatory chemicals. A diet heavy in industrial, factory-farm corn, wheat, meat and dairy may over time aggravate systemic inflammation. Wide-scale epidemics of diabetes, heart disease, kidney disease, arthritis and obesity have paralleled the growth of factory farms, as studies are beginning to show. We need to take a critical look at what causes so many people in developed countries to be fat, dull, and pained.

Individuality — Every farm is individual. Every person who works the land is individual. No one solution or approach fits all land and all people. This diversity is a strength.

Individuals — Every decision we make about food has personal and global repercussions. By now most of us understand that the food we eat may actually be making us sick. But other environmental, political, cultural, and social consequences also arise from our food choices.

Eating is an act of communion with the Earth. Preparing and eating food nourishes our bodies and rejuvenates our spirits. An unbreakable thread extends from the morsels of food we chew back through the hands of people who prepared the food, purchased the food, and grew the food, to the life in the soil that fed the plant or animal we chew.

Landscape — The landscape of a farm or garden encourages the human spirit, especially in high-stress urban and suburban environments. A farm is a counterpoint to the soul-deadening environment of congested traffic, strip malls, and vast cityscapes. Sustainable local growers can (and often do) establish radiantly healthy fields, forests, and streams, bringing warmth and hope to people who behold such fertility.

Labor — Farming is a complex task requiring tremendous intelligence, skill and strength. Farmers serve as our ambassadors to the land. Because so many of us work in offices or factories and see the land through a window, farmers touch the Earth for us. We need to actively support our emissaries and cultivate their intelligence and skill.

Agrarian labor can benefit both the body and the soul, superior in many ways to a jog or a workout at the gym. Honest agrarian work connects people with the land that sustains them, and yields value for family and community. A just and effective agrarian ethic must recognize that people who produce our food should be compensated fairly for their work. Those who do the work so everyone can eat must share in society's bounty.

As of 2009, roughly three million human beings serve as migrant and seasonal farm workers in the US. Farm workers are racially and culturally diverse. They are typically poor and live in substandard housing, where they endure low literacy, lack primary health care, and low social status. Our agricultural status quo rests uneasily upon the workers' backbones — backbones we enlist when we vote with our dollars at the grocery store. Here is a key ethical question: How do we treat our fellow human beings who undertake the toil to feed us all?

Local — Producing food locally reduces transportation costs. In the conventional food system, the average meal may travel about 1,500 miles, whereas with local food systems, the average meal travels 45 miles. The energy savings are enormous. By strengthening local economies with the capacity to produce our own food, plus a surplus for market, we attain economic, environmental, and agrarian advantages that produce benefits on a vast, networked scale.

Native Roots — Though the word *ethos* originated on another continent, the concept it denotes has deep roots on Turtle Island (North America). A basic idea was to honor both the above and the below, as well as every element in the Sacred Hoop of life. The core traditions of the continent recognized not only a sky father meriting respect, but also an Earth mother who gives us food, clothing, shelter, and beauty. In return, we must take care of her.

In 1851, Chief Seattle eloquently expressed core aspects of the native ethos: "Every part of this Earth is sacred to my people. Every shining pine needle, every sandy shore, every mist in the dark woods, every clearing and humming insect is holy in the memory and experience of my people...Teach your children what we have taught our children that the Earth is our mother. Whatever befalls the Earth befalls the sons of Earth...this we know; the Earth does not belong to man; man belongs to the Earth. This we know. All things are connected like the blood which unites one family. All things are connected."

Another foundational native concept is the Seventh Generation, an understanding that encourages human beings to work with continual awareness of, and for the benefit of, the seventh generation of children who will be born in the future. "In every deliberation we must consider the impact on the seventh generation." By keeping our children in mind, we tend to make careful and wise decisions.

Being native to place means to live as if you're there for the long haul, to take care of the land as if your life and inner peace depended on it. They do.

Nature — If we regard the natural world as an object — constellations of soulless material — then we may, as many have done, exploit everything for profit and power. The harsh, inevitable consequences of this exploitation could destroy the basis of our life on Earth. If, instead, we approach the natural world as an expression of life and see ourselves as caretakers committed to an agrarian ethos, then we strengthen and enhance the basis of our life.

Ownership — Crucial to our future and the health of both our soils and souls is the question of how we will relate to the land: as conquerors and subjugators, or as relatives who recognize our dependence upon the land for life and growth, and act accordingly.

Ultimately, agrarians must consider the questions surrounding the ownership of and access to land. Every human being has a legitimate interest, and a basic and unavoidable need, to draw sustenance from the land. Thus, we must strive for a more equitable legal relationship with the land.

"We abuse land because we regard it as a commodity belonging to us. When we see land as a community to which we belong, we may begin to use it with love and respect." ~ Also Leopold

A host of extreme difficulties arises from the practice of using land as collateral for debt, placing it under the burden of a mortgage. Under this system the bank must be paid every month and every year, no matter the weather or market conditions faced by the farmers. As a consequence, the onus of farm debt has driven thousands of families from their homes and caretaking the Earth.

Because land is the basis of our physical existence, we need a new approach to the way we hold and steward the land. One possibility that's been steadily gaining ground is to gradually protect agricultural land through legal, free-will land trusts. To do this, farmland is purchased for the last time, and then placed into forms of trust that protect it from ever again being mortgaged or sold for private profit. These trusts can make land available to qualified people who will provide wholesome food for the community and establish oases of radiant environmental health.

Landowners themselves could form such trusts, or groups of citizens could cooperate locally to purchase available land for ecologically sound farming. This cannot be legislated or otherwise imposed. To be acceptable, every step of progress should arise from the free, honest initiative of the people.

Precautionary Principle — This is the widely respected basic idea that we should, in all activities, respect the life and integrity of the land. This safeguarding principle is often expressed as "better safe than sorry." The Precautionary Principle mirrors the ethical statement "Do no harm" that still guides modern medical doctors as part of the Hippocratic Oath.

Our food can and should be produced without harming the environment and in a way that enhances the land — creating a network of environmental oases that radiate good health to the surrounding countryside.

When we support and enhance the land, we enrich ourselves. On our collective behalf, farmers have direct responsibility for care of the land and all the creatures: chickens, cows, sheep, hogs, and other animal relatives we eat to sustain our lives. We have a direct responsibility to support farmers so they do not harm the land in our name, but instead bring it to maximum health and fertility.

Quality — By focusing on quality as well as quantity, farmers have an opportunity to uplift the cleanliness, vitality, and nutritional value of our food, thereby empowering the health, strength, intelligence, and will of the people. When we strive to extract sheer tonnage of edible matter from depleted soils by pouring on imported, chemical-based fertility, we are not bolstering food-value or quality. Evidence is mounting that a clean, organic diet is more nutritious than chemical-based, processed food, and helps lengthen our lives by addressing the huge problems of obesity and diabetes.

Rhythm — Our human life is interwoven with the life of the Earth. Our food, water, clothing, and shelter come from her body and depend upon her natural rhythms. Our skin and bones are formed of her stuff. Our moods, thoughts, and capacities are not wholly independent of this relationship.

A rhythm is a cyclic process connected, not to a theoretical or artificial division, but to something real: the waxing and waning moon, the Earth's revolution around the sun, our in-breath and out-breath, and even our digestion. Our bodies, minds and spirits react in measurable ways to cycles such as day and night, and the seasons. Subtle inner rhythms in both planet and person mirror the level of harmony or discord in a life. The land underlies all this.

The basic pattern of a rhythm is simple enough: activity-rest/activity-rest/activity-rest. Yet distinctions, variations, tones, permutations, and counterpoints exist. In a healthy agrarian context, we note distinctions in the natural rhythms of the land by celebrations: planting festivals, harvest festivals, thanksgiving festivals, fairs, and so forth — all natural to the life of a healthy community. The festivals give something intangible and important back to the land in return for all she gives to us.

As Earth has a rhythm, so do all creations that inhabit her. Those rhythms are related. To remember this relationship and acknowledge it is to invite health, vitality, and balance into our lives — and to offer it back to the land.

Rights and Responsibilities — If we assume rights to the land, we must also accept responsibilities.

Seeds — Seeds are more than a source of food; they are a living expression of human life. They carry the experience and wisdom of the land to our bodies and nervous systems. Natural, open-pollinated seeds embody this wisdom, having been domesticated over more than 10,000 years.

A key element in our transition to post-fossil-fuel food production should be to relearn the art of seed saving. The current system for producing and distributing seeds is vulnerable to problems associated with hybrids and genetically engineered food crops, and dependence on our current transportation system. Organic farming and gardening lend themselves to conserving seed.

Soil — A handful of the land — of soil — contains dozens of species of microscopic life, and billions of individual organisms. These living organisms are essential to the land's health and the production of healthy, clean food. The soil is alive with springtails, fungi, bacteria, Earthworms, and more. Because the soil itself is literally alive, it merits the same respect and honor as any living being. While chemical agriculture tends to inhibit or distort the life of these organisms, organic agriculture nourishes and enhances it.

Stewardship — England's Prince Charles has noted that human beings accept stewardship for the Earth under a sacred trust. This idea is common to most spiritual traditions, he said, and is embraced in broader terms by many atheists. He urged the people of the world to recapture a sense of the sacred, in which we accept the bounds of balance, order, and harmony in the natural world, and recognize that development is progress only when it is sustainable.

We have an opportunity to take our husbandry skills and practices many notches higher as we apply creative intelligence. Guided by an ethos of respectful stewardship, we can and will continue to develop clean, innovative techniques and technologies to sustain the land and ourselves.

Chapter Three
Citizen Responses

Amid the turbulence of transition, small actions may have major cumulative effects. We stand at a moment of unparalleled creative opportunity, when engaged citizens can respond to the call of the land directly and meaningfully through a range of emerging agrarian visions and models.

The immense challenges we face arise from the sum of countless everyday choices about what to buy and what to eat. Therefore, beginning at the level of individual households, we have an opportunity to transform our relationship to the land by becoming neighborhood agrarians. The collective impact of our individual actions can become public solutions.

During World War II, Victory Gardens produced more than 40 percent of America's vegetable diet. That's a lot of food. If we put our minds and hands to the task now, we could produce even more, meanwhile enriching the health of our land, saving money, and ensuring clean food for our families.

Eating and farming are both agrarian acts. Every dollar we spend at the grocery store is a vote for the kind of food and farms we will have and the character of our relationship with the land: destructive, or nurturing.

Generations ago the famous epicure Anthelme Brillat-Savarin opined, "You are what you eat." That observation reminds us that everything we take into our bodies becomes the building blocks of our cells, tissues, and body fluids, and impacts our mental and emotional state. What are we becoming when we eat processed food products grown from genetically engineered seeds in a slurry of petrochemical fertilizers and pesticides, and preserved with either synthetic chemical substances or irradiation? And what do the ubiquitous high-fructose corn syrup, and the encroaching reality of mass-produced cloned meat add to that base?

As citizens, we can make our own choices — choices that influence everyone's future. By producing, distributing, purchasing and eating food of real quality we can help save the world.

This chapter explores agrarian visions and practices on the scale of individual homes and neighborhoods. What follows is a sample of responses, ideas and models that can turn things around and make a difference.

Locavore — Sometimes called the 100-mile diet, Locavores strive to obtain their food from within a 100-mile radius of their homes. This concept makes good sense for much of the world.

Individual dietary changes can accomplish at least five key things: support local growers and ranchers, save fuel needed to transport food over long distances, cut pollution, improve the soil, and improve health.

Eating in season gives us fresher, more nutritious foods. This also helps check suburban sprawl and keeps some autonomy in food sources. It saves energy and therefore helps prevent climate change.

The UN's Food and Agriculture Organization (FAO) estimates meat production accounts for nearly a fifth of global greenhouse gas emissions. Thus, if people want to take effective personal action to help tackle climate change, they could have one or more meat-free days each week. This is the advice of the United Nations Intergovernmental Panel on Climate Change. The panel argues this diet change has become important because of the huge greenhouse gas emissions and other environmental problems — including habitat destruction — associated with rearing cattle and other animals.

As observed by Sharon Astyk, co-author of *A Nation of Farmers*, suburbia occupies vast swaths of former prime farmland. NASA's ecological forecasting research group reports that the people living in suburbia already water about 30 million acres of lawn, three times the land planted in irrigated corn. Those well-watered lawns average somewhere between one-fifth and one-third of an acre in size. Gardening authorities like John Jeavons and Gene Logsdon point out this represents an ample plot for growing family food. Consequently, people living in the suburbs are in many respects ideally positioned to become small-scale farmers — neighborhood agrarians — right where they are. This reality may turn out to be a silver lining to suburban sprawl.

Growing a goodly portion of one's own food can be a cornerstone of sound household economy for many people who now participate only in the demand side of agriculture.

Steve Diver, a consultant for Sustainable Growth Texas observed, "With peak oil, unstable economy, and climate change — people are wondering how to get by. I see a big part of the answer as self-sufficiency and sustainability...

"As an agricultural specialist now working with farmers and gardeners, I teach them how to do food production. I have learned that it takes time to get the skills and tools, and to improve the soil. Realistically, it takes about three years to get a new garden together.

"One thing I have developed over the last 10 years is an appreciation of the whole system of production around a ¼ acre garden. It turns out the dacha gardens in Russia are typically about a ¼ acre in size, and also the gardens under old serf system in Medieval times were that size. As it turns out, that's a good size for a 'country garden' — about 104 feet long, by 104 feet wide. With a garden that size you can grow corn, okra, green beans, potatoes, beets, etc. That kind of garden requires a lot of work, but it can feed a family of four or five people.

"Also consider the combination of small raised-bed gardens, along with container gardening. Adding expanded shale to your soil makes a big difference in a hot, arid climate because it retains moisture. You can get it at local nurseries.

"You can really stretch your normal thinking about what containers are, window flower boxes with herbs and vegetables. Round plastic saucers that people normally put under pots are also useful. Find the biggest 20 inches, they are only two or three inches deep, but fill and load up with lettuce spinach and bok choy, for example. That whole process plays up in shallow-bed technique. Unless dealing with tomatoes, or peppers, many things only need two or three inches of root space — roots grow horizontally."

"Another thing is food preservation: putting up food. That's a very solid idea, although in a busy, industrial culture, people do not have a lot of time for food preservation. But there are other ways. You freeze food, or dry it for the off season."

American Community Gardening Association — The American Community Gardening Association (ACGA) is a nonprofit membership group of professionals, volunteers and supporters of community greening. The Association says community gardening improves our quality of life by providing a catalyst for neighborhood and community development, stimulating social interaction, encouraging self-reliance, beautifying neighborhoods, producing nutritious food, reducing family food budgets, conserving resources and creating opportunities for recreation, exercise, therapy and education. ACGA promotes and supports all aspects of community food and ornamental gardening, urban forestry, preservation and management of open space, and the management of urban, suburban, and rural lands.

Square Foot Gardening — During a time of global transition, when people may need to live on what they can produce, the system of raised-bed gardening known as Square Foot Gardening could become an important survival practice for many families. The simple system requires little in the way of training, and has many appealing attributes.

- No heavy digging, tilling, or weeding
- Can be implemented virtually anywhere, whether urban, suburban, or rural. Soil is not an issue. Traditional gardening usually takes several years to condition the soil. Square Foot Gardening replaces unsuitable or depleted soil with an easily prepared soil mixture, giving immediate results.
- Highly productive in a small space
- Water efficient
- Your own compost furnishes the nutrients rather that store-bought, chemical-based fertilizers. Compost is renewable and sustainable.

Lawn Transformation — The book *Food Not Lawns: How to Turn Your Yard into a Garden, and your Neighborhood into a Community* by Heather Flores combines practical wisdom on ecological design and community-building with a fresh perspective on an age-old subject. An activist and urban gardener, Flores shares her nine-step permaculture design to help farmsteaders and city dwellers alike build fertile soil, promote biodiversity, and increase natural habitat in their own "paradise gardens."

This permaculture lifestyle manual inspires readers to apply the principles of the paradise garden—simplicity, resourcefulness, creativity, mindfulness, and community—to all aspects of life. Some permaculture ideas are to plant "guerilla gardens," preparing the soil and sowing seed in barren intersections and medians; and to work with children to create garden play spaces.

Flores' book argues that growing food where you live is a key method of becoming a food activist in the community. The book promotes small, easy changes in lifestyle, and offers an extensive list of resources.

While people have been growing food in their backyards forever, front-yard vegetable gardens are a newer opportunity for people whose backyards are too shady or too small. The topic has drawn more interest as bloggers chronicle their experiences and environmentalists scrutinize the effects of chemicals and water used to grow lawns. *Food Not Lawns* has inspired many people to dig up their front lawns and plant productive gardens, with vegetables, herbs, flowers and salad greens — a source of food, a topic of conversation with the neighbors, and a political statement.

Landshare is a scheme based in England which has potential to be emulated more widely. This elegant concept puts people with large unused gardens in touch with gardeners who want space to grow food. It's a simple idea. People register their interest as a grower, a spotter (someone who notices nearby land suitable for growing) or an owner. The online register puts people in touch with each other. Participants use Landshare to find land where they can grow their own food, to offer land in return for produce, to identify land suitable for planting, and to build community.

Sharing Backyards in Vancouver, British Columbia is a program similar to Landshare. The program recognizes one of the biggest barriers to growing food in the city is access to land — despite the fact that many yards, lawns, and backyards have plenty of room to spare. Sharing Backyards links property owners who have unused yard space to people who need a place to grow food.

Permaculture — Begun in the 1970s under the guidance of Australians Bill Mollison and David Holmgren, permaculture is a system of self-sufficient gardening that married the concepts of "permanent" and "agriculture" to create a sustainable approach that set roots down in America and around the world.

According to permaculture design principles, the only ethical decision is to take responsibility for our own existence and that of our children. From this foundation, Mollison, Holmgren, and others developed an approach to designing human settlements that mimics the structure and relationships found in nature. Key permaculture concepts include: placing an emphasis on diversity and using compatible perennial plants specifically adapted to local climate, landscape, and soil conditions.

The book *Gaia's Garden — A Guide to Home-Scale Permaculture* by Toby Hemenway applies the principles of permaculture to a home-scale. Nothing about this approach to gardening is technical, intrusive, secretive, or expensive. The book can help homeowners establish a lush backyard garden filled with edible flowers, bursting with fruit and berries, and carpeted with herbs and salad greens. The plants are grouped in natural communities, with each species intended to help build soil, deter pests, store nutrients, and attract beneficial insects.

Winter Gardens — Another noteworthy development for householders is year-round gardening with cold frames and hoop houses. This simple system was pioneered and popularized by Eliot Coleman in his book *Four Season Harvest: Organic Vegetables from Your Home Garden All Year Long.*

Gardeners everywhere in North America can extend the season to year-round vegetable production without an expensive greenhouse or indoor light garden set-up. In his book Coleman shows homeowners how to use the winter sun to raise a wide variety of traditional winter vegetables in backyard cold frames and plastic covered tunnel greenhouses. These constructions require no supplementary heat.

Specifically, Coleman combines succession planting (small sowings three or more times, rather than one big endeavor) with cold-frame growing in the winter months. He includes how-to instructions for building simple cold-frames. The book concludes with an extensive chapter on vegetables that survive and thrive through the winter under simple, adapted cold frames.

This synthesized approach to four-season gardening is important, innovative, and can be scaled up or down. Many Internet sites explain the principles and practices in detail, and some offer plans for constructing winter gardens. A search of the Internet will also reveal businesses that build and ship complete kits for assembling winter gardens.

Save Seeds — The Seed Keepers email list is a forum for people who study and practice techniques for keeping natural, open-pollinated seeds. Unlike hybrids or genetically engineered seeds, natural seeds reproduce true to form year after year. All are welcome to join this email list to exchange ideas, skills and harvested seeds.

Neighborhood CSAs — Woody Wodraska, farmer and author of *Deep Gardening*, has explored the concept of micro-scale neighborhood CSAs (Community Supported Agriculture). "We need many, many more gardens and gardeners, everywhere," Woody told me. "Consider what happened in Cuba when they faced a food crisis in the 1990s. Gardens sprang up on every vacant lot in Havana, once the subsidized fuel and fertilizer was shut off when the Soviet Union imploded. People grew for the community of family and neighbors, putting the gardens right there where the people lived." (Chapter 4 offers a more complete description of CSA, a model easily scaled to the size of a neighborhood, a church, a company, or to meet the needs of urban, suburban and rural communities.)

Container Gardening — The concept of container gardening existed in antiquity, probably developed by the Egyptians and Romans. Today, this is a perfect solution for people who live in cities or apartment buildings without access to a lawn or other plot of land.

Containers give gardeners the flexibility to enjoy plants in areas where a traditional garden is awkward or impossible. Even with limited space in an apartment, shrubs, fruits, vegetables, and flowers can be grown just about anywhere. Plants will thrive on rooftops, decks, balconies, stairs and even on the stoop of a mobile home.

Plants in containers can be moved easily. Whether you're shifting pots of gardenias from the front porch to the back door during the cold season or transporting them to a new home, plants in containers are inherently mobile.

Credit Unions — After successive years of bad weather during the mid-19th Century, European farmers needed a way to save their farms from foreclosure by urban banks. To do this they formed groups to pool their savings and lend money to each other. Thus began the development of credit unions.

The first credit union in the US was organized in 1909. However, it took a severe drought, the Great Depression, and the courage of President Franklin D. Roosevelt to create the Federal Credit Union Act of 1934. Credit Unions continue to be cooperatives of individuals with a common bond who save their money and make loans. Credit Unions are member-owned, not-for-profit institutions, with deposits Federally insured for up to $100,000 by the National Credit Union Administration.

One new twist on this is the emergence of The Permaculture Credit Union (PCU), which pools financial resources of people who believe in the ethics of permaculture — care of the Earth, care of people, and reinvestment of surplus for the betterment of both. The PCU applies these financial resources to Earth-friendly and socially responsible loans and investments.

PCU is composed of members who made a decision to invest their money in a financial institution that follows a code of ethics rather than the common investment practice of only considering the bottom line. They invest their funds in their local communities.

PCU employs a unique strategy of combining conservative financial practice with Earth-care ethics to supply members with a set of financial services such as share (savings) accounts, sustainability discounts, credit cards, and signature, share-secured, home-equity, and vehicle loans. Anyone can become a member of the PCU as long as they agree with the ethics of permaculture, have completed a recognized permaculture design course, or belong to an affiliated institute.

All money for the operation of the PCU comes from interest on loans, investments, and donations. They charge fees for some services, and also pay out dividends on share (savings) accounts and share certificates. Surplus funds are distributed to members in the form of dividends.

Plant a Row for the Hungry — The Food Depot in Santa Fe, New Mexico encourages home gardeners to plant an extra row in their backyard gardens and to donate the produce to the food bank for distribution to people in need. Once the produce is harvested, caring gardeners drop off donations at The Food Depot, or call the food bank for the name of an emergency food pantry or soup kitchen near their home.

Santa Fe's Food Depot is one of many food banks or other institutions that embrace the "plant a row for the hungry" concept, and create a bridge between people who are hungry and those who tend gardens. The concept originated in Anchorage, Alaska, suggested by Jeff Lowenfels in one of his newspaper columns on gardening. He is a former president of the Garden Writers Association, and that group picked up on his idea and began seeding it across America, where it has taken root.

Food banks furnish healthy nutritious food for their partner agencies and those in need. While they pick up produce from grocery stores, the farmers market and local farmers, they typically don't receive enough produce to meet the growing need. At the same time, the cost of procuring good produce continues to rise due to increased fuel prices. Plant a Row for the Hungry offers a simple way for gardeners to help hungry people in their communities.

Backyard Grain — Homeowners can grow small but significant amounts of grain in their yards, including wheat, oats, rye, barley, amaranth, and quinoa, and then use those grains to help feed their families. Backyard grains not only yield rich, delicious food, but also enhance the landscape with the beauty of grain stalks dancing with the wind.

You can search the Internet to find out specific information on growing various grains, and then judge which options are best suited for your locale. The book *Small-Scale Grain Raising* by Gene Logsdon is a worthwhile reference. Logsdon's book was published in the 1970s to help a new generation of back-to-the-land homesteaders grow and process their own grains. When interest in Logsdon's work swelled due to the recent surge of interest in sustainable food, Chelsea Green published a revised second edition with updates from the author.

Edible rooftops — The usual flat-topped city rooftop can often be transformed into a garden, an elevated platform for growing food. City Farmer, Canada's Office of Urban Agriculture, suggests many good reasons to explore the concept of rooftop gardens: they support urban food production, increase access to outdoor green space at home or at work, delay storm water runoff, improve air quality, reduce CO_2 emissions, insulate buildings, and increase habitat for birds.

Switzerland recently passed a law that new buildings must be designed to relocate the green space covered by the building's footprint to their roofs. Even existing buildings — including historical sites — must now green 20 percent of their rooftops.

Urban Homesteading — The Dervaes Family of Pasadena, California grows 6,000 pounds of food per season organically on just 1/5 of an acre of land. Since the mid 1980s, all five members of the family have worked steadily at transforming their ordinary city lot into an organic permaculture garden supplying them with food all year round. The family also run Dervaes Gardens, a successful business that offers salad greens to local restaurants. This helps fund new equipment such as solar panels, energy efficient appliances, and a biodiesel processor to further decrease their homestead's reliance on non-renewable resources.

Founded by Jules Dervaes in 2001, Path to Freedom is a grassroots, family operated, viable urban homesteading project established to promote a simpler and more fulfilling lifestyle and reduce one family's footprint on the Earth's dwindling resources. The family regards their 1/5 acre urban homestead as a sustainable living resource center where they set out to live by example, while also inspiring others.

On their website, PathtoFreedom.com, the Dervaes family writes about the changes they've already made to their lives. The website was designed by and is maintained by members of the Dervaes family as a non-commercial, home-based effort with no commercial advertising.

The family's Pasadena yard supports over 350 varieties of edible and useful plants, and they grow over 6,000 pounds of organic produce annually. This provides fresh vegetables and fruit for the family, plus a source of income. The Dervaes family farmers share their urban homestead with a menagerie of animals — chickens, ducks, two rescued cats, red wiggler worms (to compost garbage) and two goats. *Homegrown* is a documentary film, available on DVD, about the Dervaes family (see resources).

Chapter Four
Community Responses

"Heroes are people who say: This is my community, and it's my responsibility to make it better." ~ Tom McCall ~

A perfect storm of economic, environmental, and agricultural crises has prompted many families to take positive agrarian steps. But the scale of the problems is beyond one person or one household. Only neighborhood and community responses have the potential to create a wholesome new economic and cultural foundation. We *can* take care of our Earth by changing our relationship to the land and the way we raise our food.

There is no one, all-encompassing solution to the problems of our land. Multiple solutions are needed in cities, suburbs, villages, and across the farmlands. Sustainable, self-reliant systems call for community interest and the investment of community labor and capital. In return they will yield clean food, dignified work in nature, and landscapes of abundance, beauty, and environmental health.

Sometimes spoken of as "food patriotism," the local food movement is a collaborative effort to build regionally based, self-reliant food economies. It's a reaction to the global industrial models where producers and consumers are separated by a chain of processors, shippers, and retailers. Developing local food systems goes beyond environmental impact — it's also about the social and economic benefits of local relationships. This in turn leads to better farming practices and higher quality food.

Since we all need to eat every day, a small change in the way we produce and market our food will have a profound effect on human health, land health, and cultural health.

What follows is a sample of agrarian models we can replicate in our communities:

Farmers Markets — In recent years farmers markets have surged in number and sophistication, contributing their bounty to local economies. In 2008, 4,700 farmers markets were held in the USA, and thousands more in Canada. These entertaining and helpful events allow local food and craft producers to trade directly with their neighbors. This is a key, for farmers are temperamentally geared to growing food, not marketing. Farmers markets create a venue for direct transactions between growers and eaters.

These community markets are the only outlets for many organic growers, providing an important source of income and immediate cash in hand. Many communities want farmers markets, but can't find enough growers to participate.

To succeed, farmers markets must be well organized. When communities create a foundation, or a "Friends of the Farmers Market" group, they tend to prosper from this strong support base.

The farmers market movement has established deep roots in Seattle, Washington, with five weekly markets around the city, and the Pike Place Market open seven days a week. Truck farms from 10 to 100 acres located near the city have become profitable for the first time in many decades.

Santa Fe, New Mexico has recently built a permanent, year-round farmers market building, using sustainable methods, so local growers have a place to bring food every month throughout the year. The availability of the market in a busy city district will encourage local growers to cultivate winter gardens to produce greens, and construct cellars for storing root crops like beets, potatoes, turnips and carrots.

Urban Agrarianism — As stated in a 2008 report from the European Commission's Joint Research Centre, more than half the world's population lives less than one hour from a major city, and 95% of the world's population is concentrated on just 10% of the land. We reached this point earlier than predicted, and urban agriculture has become more important than ever before.

The urban agriculture movement has grown vigorously in recent decades. The UN's Food and Agriculture Organization (FAO) selected urban agriculture as one of its main policy recommendations for the future.

When I interviewed Ben Gisin, publisher of *Touch the Soil* online magazine, he told me the two most promising agrarian possibilities are urban agriculture and systems where farmers offer direct food-security.

"We will need to grow more food in and around cities," he said. "Localizing food systems means moving producers and consumers of food closer together. It also means relying on the local manufacture and regeneration of all the elements of the production process — from seeds to tools and machinery."

Urban agriculture involves growing plants and raising animals within and around cities. Mostly international, it's just beginning to catch on in America. Crops may be grown inside cities or in adjacent lands and communities; on private land (owned, or leased) or on public land such as parks, conservation areas; or even in schoolyards or hospital grounds. Urban farm products range from vegetables, root crops, mushrooms, fruits, and grains, as well as rabbits, goats, sheep, cattle, pigs, guinea pigs, poultry and fish.

Local officials and nonprofit groups have been providing land, training and financial encouragement. But the impetus, in almost every case, has come from the farmers, who often labor when their day jobs are done.

Urban agriculture has the potential to make an important contribution to both urban food security and employment. This concept also proves fruitful in cities with weak real estate markets and declining populations. Hundreds of farmers are working in Detroit, Milwaukee, Oakland and other areas with low-income residents, high rates of obesity and diabetes, and undeveloped land.

In Detroit, food gardens are scattered through backyards, schoolyards, vacant lots, and even the floor of an abandoned factory. The number of productive plots has grown to a sprawling network of nearly 450 gardens since Detroit's Garden Resource Program Collaborative began coordinating them in 2003. The program is an effort to give hundreds of home, school and community gardens access to resources and information so they may grow, harvest, prepare, and preserve food for their families in their backyards and neighborhoods.

Wayne County, Michigan, where Detroit is located, was hit especially hard by the mortgage crisis. The county inherited thousands of unwanted properties, leaving plot after plot of vacant land. So a nonprofit group pitched an idea: Take that unused land, and grow food for the needy. In 2008 a group called Urban Farming took 20 derelict properties in the county, pulled weeds, shoveled in fresh topsoil, and planted fruits and vegetables. The gardeners grow much of the food for themselves, but they have also organized a co-op, Grown in Detroit, to sell surplus peas, onions, yams, and greens.

Detroit is 138 square miles divided between expanses of decay and emptiness and tracts of still-functioning communities and commercial areas. Close to six barren acres of an estimated 17,000 have already been turned into 500 mini-farms, demonstrating the lengths to which planners will go to make land productive. "We plan to triple that every year," said Michael Travis, deputy director of Urban Farming, a Detroit-based nonprofit corporation that helps clear land and provides topsoil and fertilizer.

City Slicker Farms in West Oakland, California started in 2001 with a quarter-acre garden and a farm stand selling neighborhood favorites like collards and mustard greens. Since then, the owners of five additional vacant lots allow the group to grow food on their land.

In Milwaukee, the nonprofit Growing Power operates a one-acre farm crammed with plastic greenhouses, compost piles, do-it-yourself contraptions, tilapia tanks and pens full of hens, ducks and goats. They grossed over $220,000 last year from the sale of lettuce, winter greens, sprouts and fish to local restaurants and consumers.

Urban farmer Will Allen was named a MacArthur Fellow in 2008. The Fellowship is a $500,000 grant for people who show exceptional creativity in their work, along with the promise to do more. Allen is transforming the cultivation, production, and delivery of healthy foods to underserved, urban populations. In 1995, while assisting neighborhood children with a gardening project in Milwaukee, Allen began developing the farming methods and educational programs that are now the hallmark of the nonprofit organization **Growing Power**. Behind all his efforts is the knowledge that limited access to affordable fruits and vegetables contributes to the unhealthy diets of low-income, urban populations, which in turn leads to health problems such as obesity and diabetes.

Through a combination of low-cost farming technologies — including use of raised beds, aquaculture, vermiculture, and heating greenhouses through composting — Growing Power produces vast amounts of food year-round at its main farming site, two acres of land inside Milwaukee's city limits.

Over the last decade, Allen expanded Growing Power's initiatives through partnerships with local organizations and activities such as the Farm-City Market Basket Program, which provides low cost baskets of fresh produce grown by members of the Rainbow Farmer's Cooperative to low-income urban residents. Growing Power's internships and workshops engage teenagers and young adults, often minorities and immigrants, in producing healthy foods for their communities. They furnish intensive, hands-on training to help people create similar farming initiatives in other cities.

In 1999, the Consultative Group on International Agricultural Research (CGIAR) launched a system-wide initiative to direct and coordinate the collective knowledge and technologies of the Future Harvest Centers towards strengthening urban agriculture. CGIAR is a strategic partnership, whose 64 members support 15 international centers, working in collaboration with hundreds of government and civil society organizations as well as private businesses around the world. Their Initiative,

Urban Harvest, helps local programs associate with national and international efforts.

Producer marketing cooperatives are a way for community-scale organic farmers to pool their resources, develop better networks, and serve regional markets.

The Relocalization Network was created by the Post Carbon Institute to address the obvious implications of peak oil. They found the most effective strategies are initiated at the community level. The network poses an inevitable question: "With peak oil relegating globalization to the dustbin of history and localization the only way that we'll be able to maintain civilization, what is the best way for your community to sustain itself?" To help people answer this question, they offer web-based communication tools to help local groups pool resources, share project templates, and collaborate on initiatives.

They support local groups who develop community programs, and also serve as working models for communities seeking ways to increase their resilience. These groups operate autonomously, while receiving guidance, educational resources, project and technical support, and electronic infrastructure from The Relocalization Network.

Small Farms are the optimum model for sustainable agriculture because diseconomies of scale occur as farm size increases. The average small farm is a polyculture, where the farmer may be growing a few acres of corn, raising several varieties of livestock, and tending an acre of vegetables. Large farms tend to be monocultures where only one crop is grown. If economists measure the total output of one crop per acre, a large farm seems more productive. But when total output of grains, fruits, vegetables, and livestock produced on a farm are measured, the small farms are more productive overall.

A 1998 report by the National Commission on Small Farms concluded that small farms are the foundation of any vibrant rural community, and the future of agriculture depends upon their re-growth across the country.

CSA — Drawing on inspiration from overseas, Community Supported Agriculture (CSA) was initiated in the US in 1986 on two farms, one in Massachusetts and one in New Hampshire. Building slowly at first and then swiftly, the number of CSAs grew through an era of general farm loss. By 2007, the USDA census estimated about 13,000 CSA farms existed across the country. These CSA farms are a simple way for people to directly involve themselves in healing of the environment, to produce clean food for their families and neighbors, and to provide dignified work.

As first conceived and practiced at many farms, CSA is not just another new approach to marketing for farmers. Rather, CSA is about renewing agriculture by linking farms with the human community that depends upon farming for survival. As a result, CSA can help us renew our human relationship with the Earth.

While CSAs confront a host of challenges and questions, they do work. These farms feed people, save energy and money, take care of the land, make it possible for people to farm the land on a sensible scale, and bring networks of independent households into direct connection with each other and the Earth.

Farms on this general model have taken root in many communities. Several variations and models of CSA are being used from neighborhood scale, to cities, suburbs, churches, and corporations. They hold great promise for the future.

Community Supported Agriculture is an economic and social association among local households and farmers who share the responsibility of producing and delivering fresh food. Households support the farm by paying an annual fee in the winter or spring, entitling them to share the season's harvest. They agree to share the fortunes of the farm, including potential weather-related losses.

Once harvesting begins, members pick up a weekly box of fresh food, which may include produce, fruits, cheeses, eggs, meats, poultry, flowers, herbs or preserves. Pick-up sites are located at a member's house or at the farm.

Marketing isn't usually a strong suit for farmers. When a group of people cover the farm's annual budget, as in CSA, growers can focus on developing the farm.

Associative Economy is another underlying concept for CSA, although not widely practiced at this time. The profits from CSAs and their variants are rarely monetary, and yet they are, I contend, more valuable than money. CSAs yield a rich harvest of social and environmental benefits that help to bring a sense of balance — a sense of the sacred — back to the essential foundation of modern civilization: farms, from whence we can support and enrich the rest of our civilization.

As Trauger Groh and I came to appreciate when we wrote *Farms of Tomorrow*, CSAs offer several distinct benefits:

- Economy — CSAs make it possible for small-scale farmers to exist and enjoy direct involvement, respect, and support from their local communities.
- Land — CSAs hold land open for farming, often through community land trusts and other cooperative mechanisms.
- Education — CSAs bring young people into direct contact with the land, and convey a whole catalog of virtues: a modest lifestyle, the importance of placing duty before pleasure, and the value of work.
- Environment — When families have a direct relationship with farms and farming, they see and care more deeply about the environment, and they want to ensure things are properly done.

• Culture — CSAs engender a healthy rhythm of community: from business and planning meetings in the dark of winter, to celebrations at planting and harvest times. Since these gatherings are centered not just on ideals, but on something real — land and food — they help weave communities together.

In the beginning, many CSAs were owned by a group of community members, each of whom purchased a share of the business. They hired a farmer who raised crops to divide among shareholders. In other CSAs a farmer with land offered shares to a church-based community or a work-based community. People buy shares up front, and in exchange receive a box of vegetables and possibly milk, meat, eggs and flowers, depending on the CSA.

But that model didn't suit everyone. In response farmers came up with different approaches to CSA. Some began offering mix and match, where the week's harvest was set out, and members could fill their baskets with whatever they chose, rather than receiving a uniform box stuffed with the same mix for all members. Other small-scale farms joined together to create a single cooperative CSA, allowing each farm to concentrate on the crops they do best, then pooling the harvests to give members a wide range of choices: not just vegetables, but also fruit, milk, meat, and eggs.

The most successful CSAs flourished with an additional twist, based on inspired thinking about the ultimate relationship between land, farmers and eaters — a relationship that includes risk and responsibility. The Temple-Wilton Community Farm in New Hampshire, for example, blurs the distinctions by calling all members *farmers* and it has remained small, with 120 families.

The Temple-Wilton Farm is a free association of people, with the goal of supporting a farm that yields life-giving food for the local community and respects the natural environment. The members are economically organized in their independent households. Out of their household incomes they cover, individually and together, the farm's operational costs. They are not legally connected, and therefore have no legal claims on each other.

All farm members agree to share the cost of the annual budget. Any farmer (member) can leave the Community Farm at the end of the year, when they've paid their part of the annual cost. If the need arises to leave the farm before the end of the year they can either pay out the rest of their pledge, or find another member to replace them.

Church-based CSAs — Some CSA farms developed relationships with churches, a network sometimes called Congregation Supported Agriculture. This is a concept that many other churches, temples, mosques, and community congregations could embrace, since the members of local churches already have a working, cooperative relationship with one another.

The National Council of the Churches of Christ Eco-Justice Program cites a Biblical reference. "In Genesis 2:15, we are called by God to till and keep the Garden. Although most Americans know little about farming, and do not directly till God's soil, we can support farmers who do so through the choices of how and where we buy our food. By involvement in the Community Supported Agriculture (CSA) movement, churches can provide a powerful ministry to the whole community, as well as God's garden. Through CSA, churches support the type of farming that cares for Creation and ensures the productivity of the land for many future generations."

Ascension Episcopal Church in Stillwater, Minnesota and the First Presbyterian Church of Stillwater contribute to the purchase of shares for two CSA farms for low-income families and a residential facility for AIDS patients.

In Upper Sand Mountain Parish, Sylvania, Alabama, 17 Methodist churches organized to offer self-sufficiency programs that conduct a gleaning program with a statewide network of volunteers and truckers who can quickly coordinate a load of fresh produce with a recipient agency. A Gardens of Plenty program supplies seeds and fertilizer to an estimated 2,000 neighbors who live off the produce and share excess with less fortunate people. They turned an abandoned church into a cannery to preserve gleaned produce for wider distribution and to provide employment. They plan to start a coop to grow, process, and sell high quality organic produce.

Workplace CSA — An increasing number of companies are forming alliances with farms to give employees a convenient source of fresh, clean food. The CSA farmers who partner with companies deliver their boxes to shareholders right at the companies where they work, saving everyone time and gas. For example, The Grinnell Regional Medical Center (GRMC) in Iowa, an 81-bed hospital, formed an alliance with the Grinnell Heritage Farm CSA.

To help the farm prepare for the growing season and pay the costs associated with planting, shareholders pay in advance for the share. GRMC recognized that writing a check for a typical $400 share might be a barrier for many employees, so the medical center paid the upfront cost and allowed employees to pay the center back through payroll deductions. Administrators reasoned this would help employees focus on their health and wellness, thereby decreasing employee need to use health insurance. As a bonus, they could support a local farm.

CSA Networking — A farm or a group of community farms may be located in an area such as the Northeast of the United States, where producing grain is difficult.

The farms need grain for their members and livestock, and so they turn to a farm in an area that grows high-quality grain. Under associative economics, a possible approach would be to formally associate with grain farmers to cover the cost per acre of the grain they grow, then share in either the benefit of an abundant crop yield, or the risk of a crop failure.

For example, Steve Warshawer of Beneficial Farms collaborates with 12 other CSA farms in New Mexico to supply a wide array of farm products for the members of each CSA. Beneficial Farms now offers storage vegetables in the winter months, and also makes dry goods available in weekly pickups. Fresh eggs and grass-fed beef can be ordered any time of year.

Madison Area Community Supported Agriculture Coalition (MACSAC), started in 1992 in Wisconsin, includes 34 networked farms serving greater Madison, Milwaukee, Dubuque, Minnesota's Twin Cities and other surrounding areas. Over 5,000 households were connected with a MACSAC CSA farm through the 2008 season.

MASCAC works to create a sustainable, locally based food system in Southern Wisconsin by promoting and supporting CSA farms, coordinating community and farmer education programs, and operating the Partner Shares Program which raises funds to subsidize CSA memberships for households on a limited income.

Coalition CSA farms offer a diversity of share options, including extended season shares, multiple shares, and special funds and payment plans to accommodate households on a tight budget. Farmers use sustainable and organic methods to produce high quality food while enriching the land.

CSA Home Delivery — With rising fuel prices farmers and consumers need to consider options such as increased efficiency of delivery routes, combining car trips, and using more fuel-efficient vehicles. A 2008 study from the Leopold Center for fuel-efficient, sustainable agriculture looked at which transportation option consumed less fuel and emitted less carbon dioxide: farmer delivery, or customer pick-up of food products.

The study found that even if all customers drove fuel-efficient vehicles, it's more efficient to have a farmer or delivery person distribute products to individual homes, rather than having the customers pick up products at centralized locations.

Food Stamps and CSAs — CSAs can make arrangements to accept food stamps. One resource for getting a CSA started, and for accepting food stamps, is Just Food in New York City. This non-profit group works with fifty CSAs in New York City. Thirty of those CSAs offer flexible payment options. Some take food stamps.

Just Food trains community groups to set up CSA programs in New York. They do outreach to farmers, maintain a pool of technical assistance experts, and match community groups to the farms. The process for a CSA to complete the applications, secure approval, get set up, and begin to accept food stamps can take eight weeks or more.

Food Bank Farms — No longer the domain of canned corn and peanut butter, food banks are preparing ready-to-eat meals, opening their own farms, and partnering with institutions such as local supermarkets and state prisons to gather and process food. They now handle much more fresh produce, which requires overhauling the way they store and distribute food. Food banks and food pantries are buying industrial-size freezers and refrigerated trucks to store food. Some opened gleaming industrial kitchens where culinary students, volunteers or convicts in work-training programs prepare meals.

The Community Farm Kitchen, a program element of the Community Farm in Ann Arbor, Michigan, supplies member families with fresh, prepared local food. Members of the Community Farm pay at the beginning of the season for a share of each week's harvest. They also have an option to join the kitchen program, in which case The Kitchen Staff collects members' vegetables at the farm each week, then washes, refrigerates, cooks, cans, or freezes the harvest. They create dishes that can be finished and served with a minimum of preparation at home, or eaten for lunch in the days ahead.

Rather than receiving their share of the harvest in the form of raw vegetables, Farm Kitchen members may go to the kitchen in Ann Arbor and collect their share in the form of home-cooked meals or ready-to-go preserved vegetables. Each week's offering is posted on the farm's Weekly Menu blog, and each Community Farm Kitchen dish comes in a tub labeled with ingredients, storage information, and serving suggestions.

Bringing CSA to people who are poor — Localharvest.org offers an option for bringing CSA shares to low-income people. Founded in 1998, LocalHarvest is now the number one informational resource for the Buy Local movement and the top place on the Internet to find information on direct marketing and family farms. The website is a directory of farms, farmers markets, and other local food sources. Their search engine helps people locate products from local sources of sustainably grown food. Their website receives 1.5 million page views per month from people interested in buying food from family farms.

SPIN Farming is a facet of the urban agriculture phenomenon developing around the world. The acronym SPIN stands for S-mall P-lot IN-tensive — an easy-to-learn farming system that can make it possible to generate income from less than one acre of land. SPIN farming has its own vocabulary, planning systems, planting methods, and marketing strategies.

Many people are exploring SPIN because it addresses two huge barriers to farming: land and capital. SPIN farming is popular with established farmers who want to diversify or downsize, and with part-time hobby farmers who want to get the most from their resources.

The SPIN method emphasizes minimal mechanization and maximum fiscal discipline and planning. Advocates claim its precise revenue formulas and organic-based techniques make it possible to gross $50,000+ from a half-acre. You don't need to own land. You can budget for and then rent a small piece of land adequate for SPIN-farming production. SPIN farming is adaptable to the city, country or suburbs, because it capitalizes on limited resources and space.

By recasting farming as a small business in a city or town, SPIN eliminates factors outside of the farmer's control, and thereby reduces the need for government support. Some farmers do it parttime, others fulltime. Some are young and just starting out, while others are older and on their third or fourth careers.

Other than a rototiller, SPIN farmers only need a push-type seeder, a few hand tools, land and seed. The land, tools, and supplies can be budgeted for during planning and then covered with produce sales.

In partnership with the Philadelphia Water Department, the Institute for Innovations in Local Farming operates Somerton Tanks Farm, a prototype sub-acre urban farm that serves as a test site for SPIN-farming. The farm has received the support of the Pennsylvania Department of Agriculture, the Philadelphia Workforce Development Corp., the City Commerce Department, the USDA Natural Resources Conservation Service, the Pennsylvania Department of Environmental Protection, and the Pennsylvania Department of Community and Economic Development.

In its first year of operation, 2003, Somerton Tanks Farm, produced $26,100 in gross sales from a half-acre of growing space during a 9-month growing season. Then, over three years of operation, Somerton Tanks Farm achieved a level of productivity and financial success many agricultural professionals claimed was impossible.

This small operational approach creates an entry point into farming, allowing people to see whether or not they have a true vocational call to the land, as well as the strength, skill, and aptitude for the hard work.

Community Food Enterprise — the Wallace Center at Winrock International, in partnership with the Training & Development Corporation, has launched an endeavor to showcase locally-owned food enterprises from around the globe. The project is funded by the Bill & Melinda Gates Foundation and the W.K. Kellogg Foundation.

Known as Community Food Enterprise: Local Success in a Global Marketplace, this campaign builds on evidence worldwide that local ownership is a fundamental building block for long-term prosperity. Market shifts in favor of local food offer small farmers and other entrepreneurs a protential path to economic security. They publish a practitioner's guide featuring 24 case studies of successful locally-owned food enterprises, as well as maintaining an online resource center for community development.

Land Trusts — Community-based land trusts help interested landowners find ways to protect their land in the face of ever-growing development pressure. They may protect land through donation and purchase, by working with landowners who wish to donate or sell conservation easements (permanent deed restrictions that prevent harmful land uses), or by acquiring land outright to maintain working farms, forests, wilderness, or for other conservation reasons.

The Land Trust Alliance — A non-profit organization based in Washington, D.C., the alliance promotes voluntary private land conservation to benefit communities and natural systems. They are the convener, strategist and representative of a substantial network of 1,700 land trusts and organizations across America.

When the Alliance was established in 1982, fewer than 450 local and state land trusts existed across the country. The first land trusts were true pioneers with little money. They formed the Alliance because they believed that sharing policy, information and training would strengthen land trusts everywhere. The Alliance represents approximately 1.5 million people as supporters and members of various land trusts. Their collective national network has conserved over 37 million acres of land.

Equity Trust in Turners Falls, Massachusetts, one member of the Alliance, helps people set up innovative land ownership models to increase community access to sustainable food systems, preserve farmland, protect its affordability for future generations, and create affordable housing. They work to form new partnerships, so farmers and communities can pursue alternative land tenure models.

The price of a farm in today's real estate market is higher than most small farmers can afford. Equity Trust helps farmers partner with a local land trust to establish a new ownership structure for the farm, a structure that allows farmers to live on and work the land and guarantee a source of good food for the community. The land trust either acquires a specialized conservation easement, or holds title to the farm's land. In both cases, Equity Trust helps place restrictions requiring the land to be actively farmed, and limiting the price for which the house and barns can be sold, to insure the farm will remain affordable to future generations of farmers.

Equity Trust has a revolving loan fund, the Equity Trust Fund. An offshoot of this is the Fund for Community Supported Agriculture, offering investment opportunities for people who want to make financing available to small farmers. The fund makes loans to farmers to support land acquisition, cover operating costs, or make capital improvements.

Coops — Cooperatives are member-owned, member-governed businesses that operate for the benefit of their members according to common principles agreed upon by the international cooperative community. In co-ops, members pool resources to bring about economic results a single person couldn't obtain. A cooperative is a business voluntarily owned by the people who use it, and operated for the benefit of its members.

Most member co-ops are consumer cooperatives, owned by the people who shop at the stores. Members exercise ownership by patronizing the store and voting in elections. The members elect a board of directors to hire, guide and evaluate the general manager who runs day to day operations.

The National Cooperative Grocers Association (NCGA) is a business services cooperative for natural food co-ops throughout the United States. NCGA helps unify natural food co-ops to optimize operational and marketing resources, strengthen purchasing power, and offer more value to co-op owners and shoppers everywhere.

Cooperative Distribution — One way to support local farmers is to set up a distribution network that will help small-scale food growers avoid making deliveries themselves. La Montanita Food-Shed Project aims to buy 60% of its food from within a 300-mile radius of Albuquerque, New Mexico to stimulate local food production. Basically, they rented a truck, hired a driver, and ran around to connect the dots and link the urban centers of Albuquerque and Santa Fe directly with local growers.

The La Montanita project helps producers move food more efficiently, getting farm products to market. They buy, resell, and also deliver for farmers who've taken their own orders. During the first year of operation, two drivers and one truck delivered over $100,000 worth of meat, eggs, milk and produce from about 30 producers.

La Montanita's Cooperative Distribution Center (CDC) is the hub of the project. This facility offers 3,000 square feet of refrigerated storage, 1,000 square feet of frozen, and 6,000 square feet of dry storage. This facility and the staff are the foundation for CDC's work with regional growers.

Steve Warshawer of Beneficial Farm was a driving force behind the creation of the CDC. He has observed, "Small farms are not going to feed the country. They don't create access for enough people, just the few who show at farmers markets. Medium-size farms are the key to the agricultural future, and those are the ones we try to foster through CDC. It saves time and gas for farmers, and helps them get their crops to market."

The Beneficial Farms Eco Label is a project of the Co-op's Trade Initiative. Originally a non-profit collaborative of farmers and ranchers, the Beneficial eco label became part of the Co-op Trade Initiative in 2007. The Beneficial Farms Eco Label assures co-op shoppers that local foods are produced in a manner consistent with sustainable farming practices.

Salvation Farming — As a cost-free resource for farmers and food sites, Salvation Farming provides volunteer crews for salvaging farm surplus and arranging storage and distribution. Surplus food goes to local emergency food sites, educational and care giving institutions, retirement communities, and the Vermont Foodbank. In 2005 Salvation Farms was created to serve Vermont's Lamoille Valley. Over the following three years their gleanings totaled over 88,000 pounds of food. Salvation Farms has been striving to create a model that can be implemented and maintained by any community. Under the auspices of the Vermont Foodbank, the project created a manual for community-based gleaning of surplus harvest.

Community Kitchen — In 2008 the Pueblo of Pojoaque in the Pojoaque Valley, New Mexico saw the Taos and Española communities just to their north prosper with commercial kitchens. That motivated them to develop a similar model in the Pojoaque Valley.

Commercial community kitchens can help small food-producing businesses start up, stabilize, and grow. The kitchens are open to the general public and small-scale food producers can rent time and space in a fully equipped commercial kitchen with ranges, freezers, ovens, juicers, and a walk-in cooler.

Some community kitchen projects also offer food-processing business workshops and one-on-one help with projects such as drawing up business plans, designing labels and marketing. In this manner, community kitchens serve as business incubators. The Pueblo is also involved in a 12-acre community farm project.

City Policy — Oakland, California has adopted a food policy that sets a 10-year mandate for growing 40 percent of the vegetables consumed by city residents within a 50-mile radius of city center.

Oakland's Office of Sustainability set clear goals: Ensure no resident experiences hunger. Maximize self-reliance and the capacity to grow and supply healthy local food through community and rooftop gardens, farmers markets, community supported agriculture, and other urban agricultural activities; promote a "closed-loop" system that uses food waste recovery while reducing energy use; promote economic development opportunities that create jobs and recirculate financial capital within the community.

County Policy — In 2007, Woodbury County, Iowa, established a community partnership designed to support the region's growing industry — The Siouxland Initiative. They declared their county the Midwest Capital of Organic Food Production & Processing.

The Siouxland Initiative then prepared a comprehensive benefits and services plan to encourage companies around the world to locate in their area. The region has been a center of food production for over 150 years, and is now embracing the organic food industry as a means to promote a wholesome food supply for the nation.

In support, Woodbury County adopted an Organics Conversion Policy that provides a five-year 100% rebate on property taxes for farmers who convert from conventional to organic farming practices.

Sioux City resolved to further develop the city's capacity for organic food processing, packaging, storage and transportation businesses. They've been processing food for generations, so the switch to organic processing is a natural response to a new era. Woodbury County is developing a farmer network chart connecting local suppliers with regional farmers; building a four-county marketing consortium for local food-based businesses; and developing a Homestead Program to offer no-interest loans to eligible farmers.

All-Organic County — Marin County in California set a goal to become the first all-organic county in the nation and create a fully integrated food system within county borders. The county is intent upon preserving farmland and farming as a way of life in the region, focused on environmental soundness and economic profitability.

Marin Organic was developed by an association of farmers, ranchers, agriculture advisors and marketing experts to serve Marin County's producers and consumers. The county's goals are supported by the UC Cooperative Extension, Office of the Agricultural Commissioner, Marin County Board of Supervisors, Marin Agricultural Land Trust, Marin Food Policy Council, and consumers.

Community Gardening — About 80 percent of the US population lives in cities or suburbs. Food travels 25 percent farther that it did in 1980, and fruits and vegetables spend up to 14 days in transit. Most fruit and vegetable varieties sold in supermarkets are selected for their capacity to withstand industrial harvesting and extended travel, not for taste or nutrition. Community gardening — no matter the makeup of the group — engenders other values.

In her book, *City Bountiful: A Century of Community Gardening In America*, Laura Lawson charts a movement that stretches back to the 1880s. Lawson says urban gardening programs have had three missions: bringing nature to the city, offering educational opportunities to low-income and immigrant children, and cultivating a self-help ethos in a democratic space. "The garden itself," Lawson writes, "is rarely the end goal, but rather facilitates agendas that reach beyond the scope of gardening."

The Community Food Security Coalition, a food policy organization with more than 200 member groups, defines urban agriculture as "the growing, processing, and distribution of food and other products through intensive plant cultivation and animal husbandry in and around cities." The coalition divides urban agriculture into commercial farms, community gardens, and backyard gardens.

Programs like Boston's Food Project have begun to collapse such distinctions. They run commercial farms, but also invest in their communities and create local supply networks. In Brooklyn, New York, a group called Added Value turned an old asphalt baseball diamond into a full-functioning farm. And in Philadelphia, Mill Creek Farm uses storm runoff to irrigate its urban farm.

Community agriculture projects are sprouting in cities across the country—Alemany Farm in San Francisco, the Massachusetts Avenue Project in Buffalo, NY, the Jones Valley Urban Farm in Birmingham, Alabama, and Urban Harvest in Houston, Texas.

These projects help people sustain themselves. Both City Slicker and Food Project run backyard gardening programs that supply wooden planters, seeds, seedlings and ongoing assistance for the life of the garden. They also offer lead testing to determine the safety of soil.

Since the program's inception in 2005, City Slicker farm in Oakland has helped build 50 gardens — not only growing clean, wholesome food, but also bringing together the residents of urban neighborhoods. To take it a step further, the produce is sold in the markets around the neighborhood and the profits go to keeping rents down, neighborhood revitalization, after-school programs, and eventually to the schools to buy supplies for local students.

Urban gardening projects usually rent land instead of trying to buy acreage at market prices. Many owners are willing to rent vacant property at small cost to benefit from the tax reductions for agricultural use. Of course, a gardening project would need to move if the landowner decided to develop the property. For that reason, it's advisable to seek a long-term lease before starting to improve the soil.

The New Agrarian Center in Cuyahoga County, Ohio studied the local food situation and estimated people within the county and their immediate neighbors spend about 7 billion dollars per year on food. Most of those food dollars leave the region, and even the state of Ohio.

Recognizing that the food choices people make have a profound impact on the future of the region, the New Agrarian Center developed a vision and action plan to help establish a stronger and more sustainable regional food system in Northeast Ohio. They intend to be part of a 21st Century food system that promotes healthy land, community, economy and human beings.

The New Agrarian Center represents yet another model of associations among rural and urban areas, where the residents confront important questions surrounding their economy and land. The Center's initiatives include the George Jones Community-Supported Farm, which emphasizes youth education and training; the City Fresh program to improve local food access for inner-city residents and businesses; and the Agrarian Learning Network to facilitate education and skill building.

The Kansas City Center for Urban Agriculture is another non-profit organization that promotes small-scale, urban food production. They sponsor the KC Community Farm, a two-acre certified organic vegetable operation with an impressive 6,000-square-foot greenhouse.

Striving to provide customers with a full range of traditional and gourmet vegetables and herbs, the KC Farm is also a demonstration and educational farm. They work with apprentices, volunteers, experienced farmers, and the general public to offer education about urban food production.

The Center for an Agricultural Economy was initiated in 2004 in Hardwick, Vermont to build upon local traditions and use community resources to develop a healthy, locallybased 21st Century food system. The Center was founded by Andrew Meyer, who owns Vermont Natural Coatings, a whey-based varnish company, and Vermont Soy, an organic soy drink and tofu company. As the son of a local dairy farmer and as a "green" entrepreneur, Andrew recognized the need to bring resources into the Hardwick area that would support value-added food products and enhance the local economy.

As the Center worked to adopt an entrepreneurial, community driven-approach to sustainable agriculture, they established a re-lending role to offer financial services, with funds going directly to local farmers and food businesses.

Prairie Crossing in Grayslake, Illinois is a conservation community designed to combine responsible development, the preservation of open land, and easy commuting by rail. The land for Prairie Crossing was purchased in 1987 by a group of neighbors who wanted to preserve open space and agricultural land. They formed a company with the goal of responsibly developing 677 acres.

Prairie Crossing made a deliberate effort to put down roots in central Lake County, making sure the landscape and architecture were inspired by the area's prairies, marshes, and farms. In the belief that community and conservation can go hand in hand, the developers and the homeowners association designed the amenities, trails, and gardens of Prairie Crossing to be places where people can meet to enjoy and care for the land.

Prairie Crossing has 359 single-family homes and 36 condominiums, all built to leading-edge standards of energy efficiency. At the heart of their development is a working farm, the 90-acre Prairie Crossing Organic Farm. The farmers grow organic vegetables, fruit, eggs, and flowers and distribute this bounty in weekly boxes to Prairie Crossing CSA members.

The Learning Farm is a program of the Prairie Crossing Institute, an educational, non-profit organization whose mission is to foster constructive, learning-based action in all areas of life, especially for environmental stewardship, sustainable growth, and organic agriculture.

Municipal Composting — Two significant environmental benefits arise from establishing composting facilities in cities, towns, and villages: the creation of rich, healthy soil for the land, and easing the expensive burden on landfills.

The Environmental Protection Agency reports that 24% of the solid waste in the US is made up of yard trimmings and food scraps. If more towns and cities had composting programs, they could convert this material into premium compost and return it to the Earth to support the growth of plants and animals. In addition to producing a saleable, organic product, community composting efforts become an important tool for diverting solid organic waste from our landfills.

Places with community-wide composting programs include Ladysmith, British Columbia, Halifax, Nova Scotia, and Rapid City, South Dakota. San Francisco has one of the most successful municipal recycling programs, where more than 63% of the city's waste, including bio-waste, was recycled in 2002. The people of San Francisco now recycle more waste than they send to landfills. For a major city, that's an extraordinary accomplishment.

To implement a municipal recycling program in a dense population center such as the Bay Area requires a sophisticated, coordinated effort. But with high fuel costs, composting food waste and other organic materials can save money and extend the life of landfills. In addition, the city generates revenue by selling a soil product for gardening and landscaping. Premium compost is a standard organic approach to enriching soil, controlling erosion, and helping plants grow bigger and stronger.

Community composting programs allow, and sometimes require, citizens to collect organic waste such as leaves, branches, grass, and other yard trimmings. The programs vary in season and structure, but they have the common goal of cycling natural material back to the land in a healthy, renewable way.

Community Fruit Tree Projects harvest unwanted fruit and have it juiced for sale as a fundraiser. For example, TreePeople — a nonprofit organization serving the Los Angeles area for over three decades — supports people who plant and care for trees on school campuses, city streets and parks, and in the mountains surrounding Los Angeles. They train people in the community to plant and care for trees, educate school children and adults about the environment, and work with government agencies on critical water issues

TreePeople volunteers have planted over two million trees in the L.A. area over the past thirty years, and pioneered more than 200 tree-planting groups worldwide. They've also initiated dozens of large-scale public and youth education programs.

In Oregon, an abundance of fruit grows on trees within the city of Portland. But every year, tons of this organic food drops without being harvested, turning into a sticky mess in yards and sidewalks. In response, starting in 2006, the all-volunteer **Portland Fruit Tree Project** began organizing people to gather fruit before it falls, and to then make it available to those who need it most. To do this, they register and map fruit and nut trees around the city in a database, then coordinate harvesting parties. They also offer workshops on pruning and fruit preservation.

Chapter Five
Systemic Responses

"Let's build a smarter planet." ~ IBM slogan ~

The term "industrial agriculture," in use for over 100 years, refers to the process whereby agricultural production ceases to be a way of life upon the land, and becomes instead a materially-focused commercial activity with monetary profit as the principal goal. That describes the status quo of our modern food system.

Global industrialization is entwined with agriculture today, just as it is with computers, banking, and automobiles. The umbrella of a mechanical-industrial mindset—efficiency and profit—has spread over the land. The consequences are vast. Like it or not, we must reckon with them.

Do we pursue the oil-driven logic of global industrialism beyond the limits of the natural world, without adjusting for environmental and economic realities? Agriculture is the human physical activity with the greatest impact on our planet. It occupies 38 percent of land, and swallows 70 percent of the fresh water. Via chemicals and runoff, it's also a massive source of pollution.

The world has a long history of theoreticians and governments rolling out agrarian reforms of one type or another to address social, economic, and environmental challenges. This book in no way calls for a particular government program to reform agricultural systems. Rather, as I and a chorus of informed observers reckon it, the land calls directly to each of us for self-directed, self-willed, cooperative, reality-guided reforms. This is an approach we human beings have not tried before, but it is open to us now, if we choose to follow that pathway.

A system is an organized collection of parts (or subsystems) integrated to accomplish an overall goal. Systems have various inputs that move through specific processes to produce certain outputs that, together, accomplish the system's goal. In this case, the system is how we feed and clothe ourselves, care for our land, and create landscapes to uplift the human soul.

Industrial agriculture is approaching a dead end. The resources that support it are either skyrocketing in cost or altogether failing. The time is auspicious for a mass, free-will guided move toward agrarian systems for a new era. Sudden, large-scale system changes can result in chaos. Yet, based on the economic and environmental facts, swift, deliberate, large-scale change is necessary. We are impelled. We have little time to respond, and we need a range of responses.

James Harrison of Boston's Food Project has observed the scene closely. "There's a certain efficiency with industrial agriculture," he told me, "and also certain inefficiencies with local, small-scale farming. What's the ideal mix between industrial and the local, sustainable agrarian movement? That's unknown, but right now it's out of whack.

"It's easy to claim that we could fully replace global, industrial agriculture. But there are a lot of people and they need a lot of food. Percentage wise, we'll see how it shakes out on a larger scale over time. Agriculture and food processing can — like all of our agrarian undertakings — be transformed. Something new can be made of it. But first we need to recognize our fundamental responsibility to nurture the land, rather than to exploit it. We must promote the life and health of the soil, and the whole ecosystem."

For decades, academics and agricultural corporations have claimed we could never feed the world from small, organic farms. But that argument has been proven wrong. Nearly half the world's food already comes from small, low-input farms of about one hectare (2.5 acres). That scale can be worked efficiently and wisely, then progressively networked with modern technology. Acre for acre, small, organic farms use less energy, create less pollution, offer more satisfying work, and produce more clean food from the land.

In the context of our overall global situation, small and midsize organic farms — the ones growing the healthiest and best-tasting food — restore the land, rather than degrading it. Diversifying crops and animals on a farm reduces uncertainty and risk from weather, market changes, and outbreaks of pests and diseases. With an integrated farming system the land yields more. Different farm activities complement each other and reduce costs.

Small farms can adapt the lessons of history, leapfrogging past the age of petrochemicals, heavy machinery and pollution, to establish farms that take advantage of solar, wind, and water power, and use composted waste to feed the land and keep it fertile. With the proper ratio of livestock, a farm organizes itself as a self-contained unit, offering an abundance and diversity of food while maintaining fertility and the capacity for future production.

Monocultures and chemical farming do not produce more food per acre. They devour energy and chemicals to produce less nutrition per acre. In fact, they use more energy than they produce as food.

The so-called "economies of scale" long used to justify factory-farming practices are largely an illusion. A 2008 report, *Putting Meat on the Table: Industrial Farm Production in America,* sponsored by the Pew Charitable Trust and Johns Hopkins Bloomberg School of Public Health, found that factory farming takes an enormous toll on human health and the environment. The report found this type of farming undermines rural America's economic stability and raises livestock in harsh conditions. The researchers called for major changes in the way corporate agriculture produces meat, milk, and eggs.

According to the Union of Concerned Scientists, most of the meat for our tables comes from "confined animal feeding operations" (CAFOs). Thousands of animals are crowded together in mass, industrial confinement, causing terrible stress for the animals and titanic heaps and pools of waste.

Traditionally a source of fertilizer to enrich the land, manure on a mass-scale has mutated into toxic waste that fouls our air, water, and land. Crowding also creates health problems for our animals, resulting in the chronic overuse of antibiotics that remain in the tissue of the meat we consume. The dubious efficiency of industrial animal production is made possible by cheap oil, cheap grain, cheap water, and cheap labor. These elements of the system are altogether unsustainable.

The report from the Union of Concerned Scientists documents billions of dollars of hidden costs the CAFOs foist onto taxpayers and communities, and the misguided government policies that enable and even encourage these practices.

Modern, environmentally sound alternatives — such as raising animals outdoors on pastures — can be a cost-effective system. Free-range, pasture-based pork and poultry are far more humane and energy efficient than confinement feeding operations.

Large corporations, from Wal-Mart to General Mills, to Kellogg, are wading into the business of organic agriculture. However, as food companies scramble to find enough organically grown ingredients, they often forsake the ethos that originally defined the organic movement. Hence, a paradox: The pioneers of clean, organic, sustainable agriculture have succeeded, but large-scale success has attracted people who may be willing to compromise ideals for the sake of monetary profit.

United Nations scientists say point blank that industrial agriculture has failed. A 2008 UN report titled *The International Assessment of Agricultural Science and Technology for Development,* painted a gloomy future for industrial farming. The report, based on a three-year study by more than 400 scientists, concluded that the world requires a radical and fundamental change in agricultural production. The technological advances of the last decades led to increased yields, but have done nothing to bring more fairness and improved nutrition to the world. The authors asserted that more value should be placed on protecting natural resources, sustainable forms of land use, regional marketing structures, and traditional knowledge.

Vandana Shiva, a physicist, environmental activist and author, observed, "The most important issue is to break the myth that safe, ecological, local, is a luxury only the rich can afford. This planet cannot afford the additional burden of more carbon dioxide, more nitrogen oxide, more toxins in our food. Our farmers cannot afford the economic burden of these useless toxic chemicals. And our bodies cannot afford the bombardment of these chemicals anymore."

Many individuals and groups are working to influence the system and move it forward in clean, sustainable directions. What follows is a sample of models that impact our systems and subsystems. Beyond this sample, hundreds of other worthy initiatives exist, and more will come into existence as conditions change.

Organic Green Revolution — Not only can clean organic agriculture feed the world, but it may be the only way to solve the growing problem of hunger in developing countries, while also addressing the severe problems with our environment and climate. A growing number of researchers, development experts, farming groups and environmentalists are calling for new emphasis on sustainable agricultural practices that make a sharp break from current policies. A 2008 Rodale Institute paper reviewing replicated research shows that the latest scientific approaches in organic agriculture offer affordable, immediately usable, and universally accessible ways to improve yields and access to nutritional food in developing countries.

According to Dr. Tim LaSalle, co-author of the report and CEO of the Rodale Institute, "When you consider that organic systems are building the health of the soil, sequestering CO_2, cleaning up the waterways, and returning more economic yield to the farmer, the argument for an Organic Green Revolution becomes overwhelming."

The data and analyses compiled in the *Organic Green Revolution* report make a compelling case that organic agricultural practices are established, commercially successful, and can be adapted to any scale of operation. This has been demonstrated repeatedly by now on spreads ranging from family market farms to commercial operations of thousands of acres. Regenerative organic techniques can adapt to virtually any location using local supplies, and transform carbon-based waste into valuable products.

Codex Alimentarius is an international organization with tremendous global power over our food and health. The Codex Alimentarius (Latin for "food code") is a collection of internationally recognized standards, codes of practice, and guidelines relating to foods, food production, and food safety. These texts are developed and maintained by the Codex Alimentarius Commission, a regulatory body established in 1963 by the Food and Agriculture Organization of the United Nations (FAO) and the World Health Organization (WHO).

The Commission's stated goals are to protect the health of consumers and ensure fair practices in the international food trade. The Codex Alimentarius is recognized by the World Trade Organization as an international reference point to resolve disputes concerning food safety and consumer protection.

Critics see Codex as a mechanism for moving the entire world toward a massive-scale, profit-based industrial approach to the land and our food supply. This compromises both our land and our food. Because its scope is global and its power far-ranging, Codex needs to re-orient itself to serve the people and the land, not monetary profit.

Environmental Commons is a broad coalition of farm, environmental, and anti-hunger groups, including the Watsonville-based California Coalition for Food and Farming. The Coalition is a statewide membership association committed to the basic human right to healthy food. They are associates of the national Community Food Security Coalition, and collaborate with communities in California to help create a socially just, ecologically and economically sustainable food supply.

American Farmland Trust — Founded in 1980 by a group of farmers and conservationists concerned about the rapid loss of the nation's farmland to development, American Farmland Trust (AFT) is a nonprofit membership organization dedicated to protecting strategic agricultural resources. Working with farmers and ranchers, political leaders and community activists, AFT has helped permanently protect more than a million acres of America's best farm and ranch land.

The Sustainable Agriculture Coalition — is a national alliance of grassroots family farm, rural, and conservation organizations from across the country. Together they advocate for federal policies and programs that will support long-term economic and environmental sustainability of agriculture, natural resources, and rural communities. This national alliance of grassroots groups takes a common position on critical federal food and agriculture policy issues and furnishes financial support for collective representation before Congress.

SAC was established in 1988 and has been deeply involved in policy education, consensus building, and policy development since that time. SAC's positions are based upon grassroots input from sustainable and organic farmers and ranchers and from private non-profit organizations working directly with farmers. SAC policy is developed through issue committees of SAC member organizations, as well as other sustainable agriculture networks and organizations.

Holistic Management International (HMI) is an international nonprofit organization based in Albuquerque, NM that offers training and consulting to stewards of large landscapes. They serve ranchers, farmers, pastoral communities, government agencies, NGOs, and environmental advocacy groups.

Since 1983, HMI has worked with people around the world to heal damaged land and increase the productivity of working lands by improving soil health and biodiversity, conserving water, reversing desertification, and positively affecting global climate change. Their approach is to train people, who will in turn educate others, about the benefits of replacing short-term, fragmented solutions with long-term systems that restore damaged land and manage healthy land. More than 30 million acres worldwide are being holistically managed.

HMI is convinced they have an effective low-tech response to climate change by addressing the problem of the CO_2 we send into the atmosphere when we burn fossil fuels and crop and forage residue. In our era, most agricultural soils are unhealthy, having lost much of their organic matter and structure. Agricultural practices that mimic nature and restore soil health also remove and store carbon from the atmosphere. HMI argues that for the land to once more sequester carbon, we must restore living soils with organic matter and abundant life forms.

Quivira Coalition — During the Spanish Colonial era in the Southwest, mapmakers used the word *Quivira* to designate unknown territory beyond the frontier. Quivira also referred to an elusive, golden dream. To help advance the dream of sustainable ranches, the Quivira Coalition initiated the New Ranch Network to deal with a range of issues: land planning, finance, livestock, marketing, management, restoration, conservation and wildlife. The Network's online directory links ranchers with helpful organizations.

The Quivira Coalition was initiated by Courtney White, author of *Revolution on the Range: The Rise of a New Ranch in the American West*. The book, and the coalition, offer guidance on how to transcend conflicts between ranchers and environmentalists to create the conditions both groups want: healthy land and vibrant communities. Courtney White says sustainable grass-based livestock systems, using management-intensive grazing, are capable of producing from 50% to 100% more protein per acre than conventional pasture/forage systems. Intensive grazing uses less fertilizer, pesticides, and fuel.

Agricultural economist Tom Dobbs believes **multifunctionality** is a model for the future, because it works on the most remote, improbable farmland. Multifunctionality is a concept that has been hidden and meagerly funded in different titles and sections of federal farm policy for more than a decade, but never been promoted as a unifying principle.

Under current federal policy, farmers receive direct payments each year, no matter what crops they grow or how they grow them. A multifunctional approach would build on and rechannel those payments, along with other crop-support subsidies, toward sustainable agriculture.

Instead of tying payments to crops and yields, they could be tied to the services farmers offer the public. Why not pay farmers to reduce synthetic fertilizers and pesticides? Pay them to enhance wildlife, diversify their crops, build soil, and restore wetlands? Pay them to develop local markets for their products, especially fresh food?

Based in Vermont's Mad River Valley, **Whole Systems Design, Inc**. is a pioneering company with an interdisciplinary team of land planners, ecologists, builders, and educators. Combining their knowledge, the designers develop sustainable homes, business, and schools by weaving together site development, landscape architecture, building construction, food production, education and other elements.

The company uses ecological design and permaculture strategies to develop buildings, landscapes, and communities that can survive climate variations such as longer droughts, hotter summers, colder winters, more intense wind and ice storms, and pest infestations. In association with clients, they explore and develop possibilities for renewable technologies, local food systems, high-efficiency building systems, passive refrigerators, solar panels, high-efficiency wood heaters, greenhouses, and edible landscapes.

According to founder Ben Falk, we need working examples of sustainable food, fuel, electricity, and mobility systems at every scale, in every valley, and every village. "If we imagine what a more regionalized and sustainable society will look like in five, 10, or 30 years, we realize that rural areas of this country are going to be pressured into performing the role that non-industrialized nations are performing today. The future success of rural societies is dependent upon the degree to which they develop regenerative working landscapes: places that produce more resources than they consume."

Greg Bowman, editor of Rodale's *New Farm* online magazine, regards carbon sequestration as a key element of system change. Carbon sequestration is the process through which carbon dioxide (CO_2) from the atmosphere is absorbed by trees, plants, and crops through photosynthesis, and then stored as carbon in biomass (tree trunks, branches, foliage and roots) and soils. A carbon sink occurs when carbon sequestration is greater than carbon releases over time.

According to Greg, "sequestering carbon is a big emphasis for us at Rodale. We know that organic farms decrease the use of petroleum, and they sequester carbon. Thus, organic agriculture offers solutions. If practiced on the planet's 3.5 billion tillable acres, organic agriculture has potential to substantially mitigate the impact of global warming."

"To change the agricultural system means changing the way we eat," according to farmer and writer Sharon Astyk. She points out that because the average farmer worldwide is a woman, and women make most decisions about what food to buy and prepare for their families, ultimately it will be women who decide whether we create a better agricultural system, or a disaster.

"Women's power as food producers needs to be recognized and empowered," she said. "The link between farmers and eaters needs to be emphasized. Farmers can't say what people are going to eat. They have to respond to consumer demand. Women do most of the shopping and cooking. They make those decisions."

Denise O'Brien, co-founder of the Women, Food & Agriculture Network, sees something similar. "We collected a lot of data. We surveyed, and found that women own nearly half the rentable farm land in the USA.

"Here in Cass County, Iowa, there are some 18,000 farm units, and women own 7,000 of them. We started to talk. We would see other women in church, lots of widows. Statistically, women live longer than men. So we did a survey, average age 65...so we look at the rest of the state — visited with over 1,000 women farmland owners to talk with them about their values concerning the land. They said they wanted conservation and natural resource management, with families living on the land. But their values are the exact opposite of what's actually happening on their land.

"If women are given the chance to make decisions about the land they own, the landscape picture can change," she said. "But many of the women are older and defer to men to make the decisions. They don't feel competent or confident, nor do they give themselves high value. So the men who rent and work the land make the decisions.

"How do women make decisions? The older generation trusts bankers and experts.

Women are not empowered to make decisions. Bringing women together in small learning circles will eventually lead to change, but it takes time."

Denise recommends mentorship. "Some women who own land could perhaps set aside 10-20 acres on a big farm to create a modest plot where young people could farm organically, and thereby give the older women who own farms a chance to express their values in the way the land is being used. If a person owns 600 acres, and sets aside 10 or 15 acres to mentor young people in a garden, not so much with practical skills, but with opportunity, there is a rich exchange."

Weaving the Web — More agricultural groups are employing the Internet in innovative ways to improve the overall system of food production and distribution.

For example, the website **LocallyGrown.net** is a pioneer in communicating with a network of farmers markets. They provide a simple system for markets to move from traditional booths-and-tables set up, to a fully coordinated, on-line ordering system. As with traditional farmers markets, growers display their goods (with digital photos) and set their own prices; likewise, customers browse through the products and buy from all or just one of the growers. All this is coordinated via the Internet. With LocallyGrown.net markets, customers usually get two full days to shop, growers don't harvest until after the order has been placed, and the customer picks up the entire order at a single location.

The system has been used by growers in Athens, Georgia for several years and is growing in popularity. LocallyGrown.net gives farmers' markets their own web address with a welcome page, a Frequently Asked Questions (FAQ) system, and a weblog (news page), all ready to go and to be personalized with individual content for each grower. If growers are certified USDA Organic or otherwise, the logo and a link for more information is prominently displayed.

Managers and growers can organize product categories, offer full descriptions, set retail and wholesale prices, post images, and so forth. They can quickly adjust prices as needed. Consumers are able to create accounts at the farmers markets of their choice. Ordering is simple. Customers can place their own orders, or market managers will place orders for customers unable to do so themselves. Confirmation emails go out to both the customer and the market managers.

While online markets can be created for free, market managers pay LocallyGrown. net three percent of their market product sales to cover site upkeep and other expenses. From there on, the market managers control other costs. Like at a traditional "booths and tables" market, the market manager may charge growers a fee to sell through the market, and they may charge customers a small yearly membership fee.

Draft Animals — A renaissance of animal-powered agriculture is one adaptive response to the global crises of economy and energy. After a long period when fuel was cheaper than horse feed, the balance is swinging the other way. Farmers are waking up to the advantages of mules, horses, and oxen that run on grain and hay, rather than expensive diesel fuel.

The percentage of North American acreage farmed by horse drawn equipment is still tiny. In one hour, a tractor can plow a hectare — an area that would take a horse all day. But farms of the future must close the fertility circle by producing much of their own fertility internally. To increase production by purchasing supplies like fertilizer increases farm costs — and farmers cooperate in their own financial destruction.

When former **Vice President Al Gore** presented his 10-year plan for sustainability, agriculture had a key role. Gore outlined a vision of clean, organic farmers and gardeners who would lead the way in developing associations, systems, and products that make their farms energy self-sufficient, while halting the direct poisoning of the land and generating clean vitality. "The planet requires it," Gore said. "The economy requires it. And our national security requires it."

New Agrarian Technology — Although we've learned a lot about growing clean, healthy food on land that is well stewarded, new tools and techniques are always emerging. If more people apply their intelligence and technological skills to the land, guided by an agrarian ethos, then more wonderful ideas and tools will emerge.

We have an opportunity to use low-impact tools based on modern, ergonomic design. We can explore thousands of 21st Century agrarian techniques and initiatives to help us better serve our land, ourselves, and the next seven generations of our children. Factories can be put to work designing and building hand tools and alternative power tools to till, cultivate, and harvest. In addition to advanced tools, many farmers already harness alternative energy sources: wind, sun, water, and energy crops.

The **Alternative Farming Systems Information Center** offers links to energy-saving tools and strategies for farms.

Chisel plow vs. turning plow and harrow. A chisel plow is a big advancement in the realm of tractor-pulled plows. It does all the work of seed-bed preparation, while leaving the top layer of soil on top, where it belongs. The chisel plow has another advantage: it does not create hardpan—a compacted layer of soil that prevents water from flowing through the capillaries of the Earth to deep roots and aquifers. This characteristic makes the plow a useful addition to limited-tillage farming, which attempts to prevent erosion by keeping organic matter and farming residue on the soil surface.

One of the projects of The Community Farm of Ann Arbor, Michigan has been the **Solar Powered Tractor.** They converted a gasoline-powered Allis-Chalmers "G" Cultivating Tractor into an electric machine, with the tractor's battery recharged by photovoltaic solar panels. The agrarian technicians describe the conversion process in detail on their website.

Though they picked the tractor conversion as their first renewable energy project, they have many other ideas for power equipment typically used on a farm: water pumps, electric fences, lights, heating, power tools, refrigerators and freezers.

Farmer Owned Coops are a time-tested way for farmers to associate for mutual benefit. One prominent example is the Organic Valley Family of Farms, which serves small farmers and rural communities by combining two business models: the family farm and the cooperative. In association with each other, they produce and market organic milk, cheese, butter, eggs, vegetables, juice, soy beverages, and meat.

Starting in 1988, seven farmers formed the Organic Valley Coop, and began cultivating so it would grow. Today, over 1200 family farms belong to Organic Valley, and share a voice in the business—because they own it. They reckon their cooperative business model has been the key to their success.

The cooperative's mission is to support rural communities by protecting the health of the family farm — working toward economic and environmental sustainability.

Lowell Reinheimer explains that his job at the coop is to help develop a new class of membership, putting crop growers into the same coop with crop buyers, thereby cultivating a form of associative economy as opposed to the market economy.

"A narrow, capitalist approach to things has in general taken over our minds," Lowell observes, "creating conditions where we no longer think critically or make rational decisions. At Organic Valley we see things differently. The market today is largely a vehicle of distortion, alternating cycles of winners and losers.

"If you want stability you have to have cooperation. If we can design a model that is workable and affordable, on the basis of free will, we don't care where the market is. This area of Wisconsin (Vernon County) has a strong tradition of cooperatives. Our fuel comes from a coop, our food from coop, even our phone service is from a coop. Our bank is a coop, too. The bank did not bat an eyelash when we went to ask for money for our business plans.

"In my work at Organic Valley, we always talk about the difficult transition from conventional to organic, from a market economy to an associative economy. But the difficult area is between the ears, the grey matter."

"When my family moved here so I could take the Organic Valley job," Lowell said, "we looked for land and we looked for people. We found a piece of land, and two partners, and went in on buying a small farm here. We're trying to create a new model for the family farmers of the future populated by people who are not blood relatives. We still have the family farm model in America, and that's also our Organic Valley mission: to preserve the family farm. But 'farm' is hard to define in our era.

"There's certainly a strong tradition where children inherit the farm, but that's an institution at risk. In my mind, it's not necessarily the ideal relationship of people to the land. There's a huge element of chance involved, and not so much willful consciousness. It seems like it often leads to neglect, or taking land for granted, not good things. None of us inherited a farm from our family, yet we are farmers called to the land. We had no choice but to associate with each other. This may be a wave of the future."

Oklahoma Food Coop — is a volunteer marketing network of hundreds of local farmers and over 2,000 shareholders — customers. Their website makes shopping convenient for people who want authentic fresh foods, but are too busy to stop at the Farmers Market. The coop only handles food and non-food products made in Oklahoma. Their business has grown at a phenomenal pace over the past few years, and reinvigorated the local food industry around greater Oklahoma City.

Association models — The Beneficial Farm and Ranch Collaborative is a trade association of family farmers and ranchers, retail stores, and consumers in Colorado and New Mexico. Participating farms and ranches tend to be less than twenty acres, and produce mixed vegetables, seed and livestock. Though licensed by the collaborative, they function as independent businesses in association with each other.

As the sustainable agriculture movements became institutionalized and uniform, the Collaborative's farmers saw a need to create a better set of standards and practices. They developed their collaborative, and a "Beneficial" label so consumers could easily find their products. The Beneficial label identifies a range of products: vegetables, eggs, fruits, meat, and prepared foods. Both producers and stores contribute a percentage of sales to sustain the Beneficial collaborative and its program.

Small-scale farmers benefit from exchanging experience and knowledge within farmers' groups. Networking for small-scale farmers who practice sustainable agriculture can go beyond the community or nation, to an international level. Just as computers simplified planning and record keeping on the farm itself, they help enormously with online networking. Undoubtedly, more agrarian networks will unfold in the years ahead.

Identifying leading farmers in each community is another way to extend the benefits of sustainable agriculture. Leading farmers are role models, helping other farmers understand the production process and environmental benefits of sustainable agriculture, so they can feel confident about changing their approach.

Chapter Six
Educational Responses

Our 18th Century transition from an agrarian economy based on human and animal labor to an industrial system based on oil and coal-fired machines required wholesale adaptation, training, and education. We're now in transition to a new order of affairs, as yet undefined. If we develop and implement individual and collective visions, 21st Century agrarianism can become the foundation for a redefined and revitalized economy, environment, and diet.

If we are to create a clean food supply, economy, and culture, then great numbers of people must become more involved with the substance of the Earth. We have too few hands on our farms. We must adapt, train and educate ourselves to travel new paths. This will take our creative intelligence, will and strength. All of this is possible.

We could put our strength and energy to work on the land instead of in gymnasiums. A one-hour workout with a shovel or a hoe can equal the health benefits of an hour on a treadmill. The shovel or hoe will produce value far beyond toned muscles.

As a matter of survival — while prices climb and supplies become less certain — we must find wise ways to move forward. That evolution must take place swiftly, and we must all become involved. A few isolated farmers struggling in the vortex of change and under the weight of mortgage debt, cannot alone take care of us all.

Agrarians Richard Hienberg, Sharon Astyk, Will Allen and others estimate that we'll need fifty to one hundred million additional farmers as available supplies of oil and gas decline. "The millions of new farmers in our future will have to include a broad mix of people reflecting our increasing diversity," Astyk observes. "Already the fastest growth in farm operators is among Hispanics, Asians, and Native Americans, as well as among female full-time farmers."

Just now, millions of young women and men clearly see what is happening to the Earth and feel deeply the call to respond by working upon the land. This human potential, coupled with emerging high-tech tools and techniques of ecological farming and the agrarian wisdom acquired from long experience, can accomplish fundamental things. It can help bring forth an abundance of clean food for people; supply dignified work in nature for thousands; and help establish oases of environmental radiance in communities all over North America.

We must apply our best and brightest creative intelligence to the agrarian challenges, pass on what we know, and enable new learning.

Farming will need to become more labor-intensive. Our Earth is so damaged that a small percentage of the population cannot stretch themselves far enough to heal our depleted land and feed all the people. Thus, we may find the new agrarians will include most of us. Eventually we may see the emergence of a new social class — the millennial agrarians: people who tend and heal the land to restore balance while feeding the people.

We need to encourage, educate, and support farmers, enabling them to respond knowledgeably and wisely to the call of the land. Not everyone is vocationally suited to work in a factory or an office. Many people are authentically called to the land — and that's where the educational response is key. Like modern-day fire fighting and engine repair, farming is a complex and sophisticated undertaking. Good farmers are made season by season, not overnight.

Universities and community colleges have the opportunity and the responsibility to develop programs in small, medium, and large-scale ecological farming methods — programs that include training in the broad range of skills farmers need.

The challenges we face and the opportunities before us require a range of educational approaches, beginning in childhood. What follows is a small sample of agrarian educational models.

Persuading children to eat good food has challenged school lunch programs for decades. Farm-to-school projects feature locally grown fruits and vegetables so fresh and flavorful that many children love them. **Farm-to-School** programs have blossomed across America, with an estimated 1,200 programs now active in 34 states, and many more in the planning stages. Schools buy farm-fresh foods, such as fruits and vegetables, eggs, honey, meat, and beans and then feature these foods on cafeteria menus. The schools also offer students experiential learning through farm visits, gardening, and recycling programs. Local farmers benefit by gaining a new market. Farm-to-school programs support local farms, improve student nutrition, and offer education opportunities around health, nutrition and agriculture. States are increasingly passing farm-to-school laws to bring food to schools.

The National Farm-to-School Program is a project of the Center for Food & Justice. Initiated in 2000, this national nrogram promotes farm-to-school programs across the United States by providing information, education, and training. On their website, they offer a wealth of resources on school gardens and the overall movement toward sustainable food systems.

In New York City, the **SchoolFood Plus** organization has brought forward many innovations. Among the most successful is a lunchroom item: a small plastic bag of sliced apples that have been grown in New York state. Since the apple slices were introduced to the menu in 2005, the city school district has devoured several million bags of them.

School Gardens are another pathway for young people to learn hands-on about where their food comes from, and to improve their diets. Across America, dozens of programs are establishing gardens inside schoolyards. Alice Waters' pioneering **Edible Schoolyard** project gives schoolchildren an opportunity to grow their own lunch, while teachers use the gardens for science and social studies lessons. Projects are thriving in Berkeley, New Orleans, and many other school districts. The Edible Schoolyard Project is an excellent model for creating organic gardening and cooking projects for children.

A growing movement has emerged to transform school lunch into a vibrant expression of education for sustainability. The Center for Ecoliteracy has launched the **Rethinking School Lunch** initiative as part of a national effort to restore the connection of farms to communities, meals to culture, and health to environment. Their programs address childhood obesity, nutrition-related illness such as diabetes, and lunch quality. The online tutorial includes a Rethinking School Lunch guide, an essay series entitled "Thinking Outside the Lunchbox," technical assistance, and grant opportunities.

California Farm-to-School program — The Community Alliance with Family Farmers brings fresh, locally grown fruits and vegetables into school cafeterias across California. As a farmer-run organization, CAFF's program focuses on creating distribution networks for school nutrition directors who wish to buy produce from local farms easily, and without increasing the school's food budget.

Growing Minds is the Appalachian Sustainable Agriculture Project's farm-to-school program. This program strives to cultivate mutually beneficial relationships between farms and schools that create dynamic, wellness-focused learning environments for children. They do this by working with farmers, educators, and communities to serve local food in schools, while expanding opportunities for farm field trips, experiential nutrition education, and school gardens. Their website includes lesson plans for teachers, and other resources.

Oklahoma Farm-to-School — Oklahoma is also active in the farm-to-school movement. The Sooner State's program began as a pilot project in 2004 with Oklahoma-grown watermelons in four school districts, then tripled in size the next year. The state legislature made Farm-to-School an official program in 2006, creating a state coordinator position within the Department of Agriculture, Food, and Forestry. Now farmers all over Oklahoma have new markets. The program brings fresh Oklahoma-grown fruits and vegetables to over 350 schools in 30 districts. Demand has consistently outpaced supply, creating opportunities for new farmers.

The Agrarian Adventure is a publicly supported nonprofit project from Tappan Middle School in Ann Arbor, Michigan. The Agrarian Adventure creates and sustains an organic school garden and greenhouse, runs an after-school enrichment program, and sponsors both a Spring Festival, and an annual Harvest Dinner, grown and prepared by youth, to share their Agrarian Adventure with their families and other people in the community.

Higher Education

Jerry R. DeWitt is an experienced voice for the land, who coordinates the Iowa Learning Farm from his position as director of the Leopold Center for Sustainable Agriculture. DeWitt helped establish the nation's first tenured organic agriculture faculty position at ISU. He also made the connection for a unique partnership between ISU and the grassroots organization Practical Farmers of Iowa, a non-profit, educational group that develops and promotes profitable, ecologically sound, and community-enhancing approaches to agriculture.

"Farmers are not just learners, but also teachers," DeWitt said. "As we move toward more sustainable agriculture, this trend is coming on. Local input will be essential.

"Community colleges and non-profit organizations around the country led the way on sustainability and organic, now some land grant schools are coming on board. Many more will. Washington State has a certificate program on organic agriculture. My own university, Iowa State, is completing development of an experimental course on organic agriculture, which may soon be delivered statewide via online technology.

"Virtually every land grant university in the nation is moving toward that. They're not necessarily leading the way, but they are reflecting a shift in awareness. We are seeing courses in organic and sustainable agriculture added to college curricula — at least at some colleges. That's a good trend. And also a heartening growth of interest in organics and permaculture.

"Courses in sustainable agriculture are a great first step, but they're not enough. For example, we have a graduate program at Iowa for about 15 students a year. But neither we nor any other university can be successful if we have both conventional agriculture and sustainable agriculture programs. The real success will be when we have just an agriculture class that has sustainability integrated. It should not be separate, but integrated."

According to Steve Diver of Sustainable Growth Texas, courses on sustainable agriculture and student activities that grow food to help feed the campus are wonderful projects for schools and colleges. He said Hendrix College in Conway, Arkansas was an early innovator in foodshed agriculture by implementing **The Hendrix Food Project**. They hired a horticulturist to get local farmers within a 75-150 mile radius of the campus to raise foods. They retrained cafeteria staff to cook with "fresh" green beans instead of "canned" green beans, etc. They published a booklet on the food project and buying food from local farmers, versus trucking it in from 1,500 miles away. Obtaining fresh produce, dairy, and meat from local farmers who must plan many months in advance takes a lot of coordination, but Hendrix College made it happen.

Another example is the **Ohio State Graduate Fellowships in Sustainability**, an educational program for graduate students interested in sustainability in relation to food, agriculture, or the environment. The core training is in the field of rural sociology, although the program encourages diverse coursework across disciplines. The fellows engage major issues of our time, including global warming, biotechnology, obesity and famine, loss of farmland, water shortages, organic and local food systems, the loss of animal species, deforestation, oil and gas supplies, and desertification.

University of Arkansas Applied Sustainability Center sees sustainability as one of the 21st Century's biggest business opportunities. In collaboration with the Dale Bumpers College of Agricultural, Food and Life Sciences, the center launched a project to identify key sustainability factors in agriculture, and also develop training modules for Wal-Mart buyers, suppliers and other decision-makers.

Yale University Program in Agrarian Studies — The Yale program is an experimental, interdisciplinary effort to reshape how a new generation of scholars understands rural life and society. Scholars from various disciplines who shaped the program agreed that analysis of agrarian development must begin with the lived experience, understanding, and values of its subjects — the people on the land.

Meanwhile, the **Yale Sustainable Food Project** was founded in 2001 by students, faculty, staff, and chef Alice Waters. The project manages an organic farm, directs a sustainable dining program on campus, and runs diverse programs that support academic inquiry related to food and agriculture. Student interns transformed a brambly acre of Farnam Gardens into a productive market garden, now known as the Yale Farm. The Farm is a place where students, staff, and area residents gather to work, to learn, and to eat. Yale's farm is a model for student farms on college campuses, as well as for market gardens in urban areas.

Tufts University New Entry Sustainable Farming Project (NESFP) was established to help people with limited resources begin farming, to support the vitality of agriculture in New England, to build economic self-reliance and food security, and to expand access to high-quality, locally-grown food. NESFP is one of the first initiatives in the United States to help immigrants and refugees develop commercial farming opportunities. They've worked with farmers from Cambodia, Laos, Malaysia, Liberia, Ghana, Cameroon, Lebanon, Colombia, Zimbabwe, Kenya, Burundi, Vietnam and Puerto Rico, among others. NESFP also offers student internships, directed study, and research. The program helps new farmers locate farmland, secure an education, develop business plans, and move into production.

In 2008, the **International Commission on Education for Sustainable Development Practice** released its final report. They concluded that no one area of knowledge can solve global hunger; this challenge calls for a multi-disciplinary approach. As a step in that direction, the Commission launched a global classroom for the study of sustainable practices online.

The Rodale Institute developed free, online organic training courses for farmers. The first of these is **The FarmSelect Transition to Organic** course, designed for farmers who are thinking about transitioning, or just beginning the transition process. The course allows farmers to fill out an Organic System Plan to evaluate how going organic might change their farm. In the online class, the Institute's farm manager walks farmers through the basics of organic production, from crop plans to weed, pest and disease control. He then introduces them to marketing, and details the record-keeping requirements for organic certification.

Worldwide Opportunities on Organic Farms is part of an effort to link volunteers with organic farmers, promote educational exchange, and build a global community. The WWOOF program started in the London in 1971. The core intention was to give city-dwellers a chance to participate in the organic farming movement taking place in the countryside. The program has expanded over the years to more than 28 countries around the world, including Canada, the US and Mexico.

WWOOF is available to anyone over age 18 — urbanites, professionals, students, families, farmers, gardeners, or people who have never touched soil in their lives are all welcome. Volunteers usually work for a half-day, participating in farm work and projects as needed. In exchange, farmers offer meals and accommodations. More than 500 host farms are listed in the WWOOF-USA Directory of Organic Farms.

4-H — With a membership of 6.5 million young people across America, 4-H supports 90,000 clubs dedicated to learning, citizenship, and life skills. The 4-H community also includes 3,500 staff members, 518,000 volunteers, and 60 million alumni. The four Hs stand for Head, Heart, Hands, and Health.

Administered by the Cooperative State Research, Education, and Extension Service (CSREES) of the USDA, 4-H'ers participate in hands-on learning activities, supported by the latest research of land-grant universities. Since its inception around the start of the 20th Century, 4-H has guided millions of young men and women toward agrarian pathways. Responding to environmental realities and emerging research, 4-H has begun offering programs and resources to help young people learn about sustainability, and has potential to do more.

The National FFA Organization — Founded in 1928 as the Future Farmers of America, the group changed its name in 1988. The National FFA Organization uses agricultural education to make a difference in the lives of elementary, middle, and high school students by developing their potential for leadership, personal growth and success. With a membership of a half a million students, NFFAO has chapters in all 50 states, Puerto Rico and the Virgin Islands. This group features some resources and programs focused on organic and sustainable agriculture, and has the potential to do much more.

Angelic Organics Learning Center was founded by biodynamic farmer John Peterson (the Farmer John of film and cookbook fame) and associates of the Angelic Organics Farm — a community-supported agriculture (CSA) enterprise in northern Illinois, with more than 1,400 shareholder families. In 1998, the farm established the Learning Center as an educational vehicle to help prepare people to farm and thereby create sustainable communities. The organization and their Learning Center are regional leaders, helping urban and rural people build local food systems. They transform the farm into a living classroom for hundreds of children, adults, and families each year, and graduates of their training programs have gone on to operate dozens of new local farms.

The Food Project in Boston, Massachusetts endeavors to cultivate a productive community of youth and adults from diverse backgrounds, working together to build a sustainable food system. They produce healthy food for residents of the city and suburbs and provide youth leadership opportunities. The Food Project's national model engages young people in personal and social change through sustainable agriculture. Each year, the program works with over a hundred teens and thousands of volunteers to farm 31 acres in rural Lincoln, and several lots in urban Boston.

They specialize in supporting a new generation of leaders by placing teens in responsible roles and giving them meaningful work. Additionally, about half of The Food Project's work involves serving as a worldwide resource center through materials, youth training, and professional development.

The project's Director of Agriculture, James Harrison, said, "One really interesting thing is having all these people who were not farmers coming into farming with their new ideas. That's such a positive thing for agriculture...As the need for food becomes greater — we will need to adjust. We're going to have to shift from educating citizens to training farmers.

"The reason we have been so successful, and that we have something to offer elsewhere," Harrison said, "is our youth development models. They encourage personal responsibility, and hard work, and youth-adult relationships around meaningful work. We emphasize the 4 Rs: Rigorous, relevant, relationships, responsibility. Another reason we are successful is that part of our mission is bringing together people from diverse races, religions, and backgrounds. You have to be able to disagree with each other. We have guidelines around the way we talk with each other, so we can disagree respectfully. That's going to be important in figuring out sustainability: that there be a place at the table for everyone."

Bioneers — Founders Kenny Ausubel and Nina Simone coined the term Bioneers in 1990 to describe an emerging culture. They and their associates define Bioneers as social and scientific innovators from all walks of life and disciplines. These are people who've peered into the heart of living systems to understand how nature operates, and then found ways to emulate "nature's operating instructions" to serve human ends without harming the web of life.

Through conferences and the news media, Bioneers established itself as a valuable source of innovative solutions. They provide a forum and social hub for education about solutions. Every October, Bioneers gathers a group of leading-edge innovators to share ideas and solutions. With more than 10,000 people attending their main conference, they use satellite to beam the proceedings to remote locations. By fostering connection, cross-pollination, and collaboration, Bioneers is a network of networks — connecting people with solutions on the local, regional, national and international levels. They also broadcast an award-winning radio series, *Bioneers: Revolution from the Heart of Nature*.

GROW BIOINTENSIVE Workshops teach an efficient method of gardening and small-scale farming based on 35 years of research. The biointensive method is being used in 130 countries around the world. Director of the Grow Biointensive Mini-Farming program for Ecology Action since 1972, John Jeavons is known internationally as a leading researcher, developer, teacher, and consultant for small-scale food production techniques. He authored the best-selling text, *How to Grow More Vegetables, Fruits, Nuts, Berries, Grains, and Other Crops Than You Ever Thought Possible On Less Land Than You Can Imagine,* a primer on sustainable Biointensive Mini-Farming.

Jeavons' sustainable food-raising methods are popular with UNICEF, Save the Children, and the Peace Corps. The comprehensive cropping system enables people in all regions of the world to grow a balanced diet on a small plot of land.

Exploring the Small Farm Dream — Cuyahoga Valley Countryside Conservancy introduced the Exploring the Small Farm Dream program to Ohio and the Midwest in 2006. This four-session business course was developed in collaboration with the New England Small Farms Institute, and extensively tested in many contexts, from New England to Virginia.

During the course, students set personal and farming goals, assess resources, determine if farming as a business is right for them, and develop an action plan to guide their next steps. This includes thinking about full-time farming, farming part-time while continuing other employment, changing careers to start a farm, taking over an existing family farm business, or developing an existing agricultural pastime into a business.

Chapter Seven
Echoing the Call

In Jack London's classic novel *The Call of the Wild,* the alpha dog Buck faces a moment of truth as he stands amid the tall pines in a northern forest. In a similar way, we humans stand individually and collectively upon the Earth facing our moment of truth. Our call is from the land.

As I hear it now, along with the other listeners chorused in this volume, the call of the land is exceedingly stark and insistent. Jared Diamond's book, *Collapse: How Societies Choose to Fail or Succeed,* offers a cogent exploration of the signs and their portents. He describes the environmental causes leading to failed societies through history and compares these with cultures that succeeded. In doing so he arrives at a blunt formula: Environmental crisis + failure of society to address = societal collapse.

When I interviewed biodynamic farmer Barbara Scott for this book, she acknowledged the crisis immediately. "We are in a collective death spiral now," she said, "but we can turn it into a collective rebirth. If we go through this historical phase of transition without a plan, and without vigorous action to make our plan real, the land will turn increasingly bitter and barren. But if we put something new into our thoughts and dreams, it will be. Our opportunity is to nourish, to encourage, and to catalyze for the future."

We stand upon the land at a juncture of choice. The pathways leading to a more damaged and increasingly unstable planet are clear. So are the pathways to a clean, healthy, sustainable future. I wrote *The Call of the Land* to articulate and echo this fact: our life-sustaining agrarian roots have immense value, but they are in grave danger if we further abuse or neglect them. With action and intelligence, we can cultivate, revive, and strengthen our roots in a way that will benefit seven generations into our future. The people and organizations cited in *The Call of the Land* offer more than philosophical ideals; they demonstrate an array of proven models that embrace an evolving agrarian ethos and that can be emulated widely.

The land calls out for a wholehearted evolution in our approach. We need to implement agrarian projects with vast networks of sustainable oases woven into every neighborhood and community, with many people directly involved. No private organization or government can do all this — certainly not with the speed and scale needed to meet our challenges. I believe the agrarian response must come not from the top down, or from the bottom up, but from a vast network of human beings who recognize the call of the land and who willingly choose an agrarian pathway.

The best and possibly the only way to ensure a healthy, sustainable future is to create it. That we can do, but the task is daunting. Natural organic farming methods are often more labor- and knowledge-intensive than industrial agriculture. Consequently, widespread adoption will require social and economic reformations.

In our response to the call of the land, everything matters. When I interviewed Shabari Lynda Bird, she said, "So much is in our thinking and our intention. Understand that when you cultivate and improve even one square foot of soil, it goes on alive and enriched for 200 years. Your name will be long forgotten, but that soil will continue to live and to heal the land for generations."

We must build a bridge that connects people to the land and to one another. We must learn to associate and cooperate with one another to attain mutual goals. This is possible. By now the technology of manifestation is well understood: Envision, set goals and objectives, assess resources, and begin to work with what you have — not what you wish you had. If we intelligently support our farms and gardens, instead of functioning as crippling sources of pollution and imbalance, they will become environmental oases, radiating health, vitality, and beauty.

Many of the voices in this book propose new agrarian visions and associations among households, farmers, gardeners, environmental organizations, schools and universities, churches, and corporations. To me, this seems essential and wise. We must find ways to marry the needs and rhythms of the land with our strength, skill, and sophisticated tools to bring the land to its fullest and most abundant potential.

A vision of space travel inspired us to walk upon the moon. Out of vision we created digital pathways that connect us globally in a vast, interactive network. Why not take another step into the vision of advanced agrarian culture? If we choose this path and follow it, we can encircle the Earth with a sustainable culture of integrity, beauty and natural prosperity. This is the vision and the potential of 21st Century agrarianism.

About the Author

A native of New England, Steven McFadden now makes his home in Santa Fe, New Mexico, where he serves as director of Chiron Communications, and continues his work as a writer, a keynote speaker, a counselor, and a healer.

Steven is the author of several other non-fiction books, including: *Legend of the Rainbow Warriors, Profiles in Wisdom, The Little Book of Native American Wisdom, Teach Us To Number Our Days*, and the epic, nonfiction saga of North America: *Odyssey of the 8th Fire*. He is co-author of *Farms of Tomorrow*, and *Farms of Tomorrow Revisited*, and has reported on the growth and development of Community Supported Agriculture (CSA) in America since its inception in 1986.

A 1975 graduate of Boston University with a degree in journalism, Steven worked in newspapers and magazines for several years before turning his hand to writing books, and to teaching business writing. He founded Chiron Communications in the 1980s, but rested the enterprise in the 1990s while he served as National Coordinator for the annual Earth Day celebration, and later as director of The Wisdom Conservancy at Merriam Hill Education Center in Greenville, New Hampshire.

A Reiki Master of long standing, he has taught the Reiki healing techniques to hundreds of students across North and Central America. He helped John Harvey Gray and Lourdes Gray, Ph.D. write *Hand to Hand: The Longest Practicing Reiki Master Tells His Story*.

Steven McFadden
Chiron Communications
P.O. Box 29662
Santa Fe, NM 87592
www.chiron-communications.com
www.thecalloftheland.com
www.8thFire.net

Resources

The Internet is vast and continually changing. Accordingly, this list represents only a contemporary sample of agrarian resources referenced in the text of this book. There may exist many more resources for any particular category, and the actual web address of any given resource may change. Please use an online search engine to find what you need.

The Agrarian Adventure
2251 E. Stadium Blvd., Ann Arbor, MI 48104
734-994-2017
www.agrarianadventure.org

Alternative Farming Systems Information Center
National Agricultural Library
10301 Baltimore Avenue, Beltsville, MD 20705
www.nal.usda.gov/afsic

American Community Gardening Association
www.communitygarden.org

American Farmland Trust
1660 L St. NW, Suite 1100, Washington, DC 20036
202-638-4725
www.farmland.org

Angelic Organics Learning Center
1547 Rockton Rd., Caledonia, IL, 61011
815-389-8455
www.csalearningcenter.org

Sharon Astyk
www.sharonastyk.com

Shabari Lynda Bird
www.wonderworkers.com

Bioneers
www.bioneers.org

CAFF Farm to School program
www.caff.org/programs/farm2school

California Coalition for Food and Farming
www.foodsecurity.org/california

The Center for an Agricultural Economy
PO Box 451 — 41 South Main Street
Hardwick, Vermont 05841
www.hardwickagriculture.org

City Farmer News
2150 Maple Street, Vancouver, BC, V6J 3T3
604-685- 5832
www.cityfarmer.info

Civil Eats
www.civileats.com

The Community Farm Kitchen
www.communityfarmkitchen.com

Community Food Enterprise
www.wallacecenter.org

Community Food Security Coalition
www.foodsecurity.org

The Consultative Group on International Agricultural Research (CGIAR)
www.cgiar.org

Container Gardening Tips
www.containergardeningtips.com

Cooperative Distribution Center
3361 Columbia NE, Albuquerque, NM 87107
877-775-2667
www.lamontanita.coop

Earth Institute Global Classroom for Sustainable Development
www.mdp.ei.columbia.edu/?id=resourcecenter

Ecological Farming Association
406 Main St., Suite 313, Watsonville, CA 95076
831-763-2111
www.eco-farm.org

Edible Schoolyard Project
www.edibleschoolyard.org

Environmental Commons
www.environmentalcommons.org

Equity Trust, Inc.
PO Box 746, Turners Falls, MA 01376
413-863-9038
www.equitytrust.org

Exploring the Small Farm Dream — A four-season course
Cuyahoga Valley Countryside Conservancy
2179 Everett Road, Peninsula, OH 44264
www.countryside.org

Farm Link
www.thefarmlandcenter.org

Farm to School
www.FarmtoSchool.org

4-H Clubs
www.4-h.org

The Food Project — Boston
www.thefoodproject.org

Food First/Institute for Food and Development Policy
398 60th Street, Oakland, CA 94618
http://www.foodfirst.org

Four Season Gardening — ivillage website
www.forums.gardenweb.com/forums/fourseason

Garden Resource Program Collaborative
Detroit Agriculture Network
200 W. Parkhurst
Detroit, MI 48203
www.detroitagriculture.org

GROW BIOINTENSIVE® Sustainable Mini-Farming
John Jeavons, 5798 Ridgewood Road, Willits, CA 95490
www.johnjeavons.info

Growing Minds
www.growing-minds.org

Growing Power
www.growingpower.org

Guidestone Farm, Colorado
www.guidestonefarm.com

Richard Heinberg
www.richardheinberg.com

Holistic Management International
www.holisticmanagement.org

Kansas City Center for Urban Agriculture
www.kccua.org

Landshare
www.landshare.channel4.com

Land Trust Alliance
www.lta.org

Leopold Center for Sustainable Agriculture — Jerry R. DeWitt
www.leopold.iastate.edu

LocallyGrown.net
www.locallygrown.net

Local Harvest
www.localharvest.org

Local Harvest CSA c/o NOFA-NH
4 Park Street, Suite 208, Concord, NH 03301
www.localharvestnh.com

Local Harvest CSA in Concord, NH has published a book entitled "Local Harvest: A Multifarm CSA Handbook."

National Agricultural Library
www.nal.usda.gov

MACSAC — Madison Area Community Supported Agriculture Coalition
PO Box 7814, Madison, WI 53707-7814
www.macsac.org

Marin Organic County
www.marinorganic.org

National Cooperative Grocers Association (NCGA)
www.ncga.coop

National Farm-to-School Online
www.farmtoschool.org

National FFA Organization (formerly Future Farmers of America)
www.ffa.org

The New Agrarian Center
www.gotthenac.org

New Ranch Network
www.newranch.net

New Entry Sustainable Farming Project (NESFP)
www.nesfp.nutrition.tufts.edu

Ohio State University
Rural Sociology Graduate Studies
www.ag.ohio-state.edu

Oklahoma Farm-to-School program
www.kerrcenter.com

Oklahoma Food Coop
www.oklahomafood.coop

The Organic Green Revolution Report
www.rodaleinstitute.org/files/GreenRevUP.pdf

Organic Consumers Association
www.organicconsumers.org

Organic Seed Alliance
P.O. Box 772, Port Townsend, WA 98368
360-385-7192
www.seedalliance.org

Organic Valley Family of Farms — CROPP Cooperative
One Organic Way, LaFarge, WI 54639
www.organicvalley.coop

Permaculture: An online beginner's guide
www.spiralseed.co.uk/permaculture

Permaculture Credit Union
P.O. Box 29300, Santa Fe, NM 87592-9300 (505) 954-3479
www.pcuonline.org/index.html

Plant a Row for the Hungry
The Garden Writers Association Foundation
10210 Leatherleaf Court, Manassas, VA 20111
www.gardenwriters.org

Practical Farmers of Iowa
www.practicalfarmers.org

Prairie Crossing — The Burnham Building
977 Harris Road, #113, Grayslake, Illinois 60030
847-548-5400
www.prairiecrossing.com

Polyface Farm — Joel Salatin
www.polyfacefarms.com

The Quivira Coalition — Courtney White
www.quiviracoalition.org

The Relocalization Network — Post Carbon Institute
6971 Sebastopol Avenue, Sebastopol, CA 95472 USA
www.relocalize.net

Portland Fruit Tree Project
www.portlandfruit.org

Rethinking School Lunch
www.ecoliteracy.org/programs/rsl

Robyn Van En Center — Fulton Center for Sustainable Living
www.csacenter.org

The Rodale Institute (TRI)
Their Transitioning to Organic training program is a 15-hour online course for
farmers who are ready to make the transition to certified organic. Rodale also
publishes The New Farm, an online magazine of sustainable practices.
611 Siegfriedale Road, Kutztown, PA 19530-9320 USA
610-683-1400
www.rodaleinstitute.org

The Sage Center
www.sagecenter.com

Salvation Farming
www.vtfoodbank.org

SARE National Outreach
10300 Baltimore Ave. — Bldg. 046 BARC-WEST
Beltsville, MD 20705-2350
301-504-6425
www.sare.org

Seeds of Change
www.seedsofchange.com

Seed Savers Exchange
www.seedsavers.org

Sharing Backyards
www.sharingbackyards.com

The Siouxland Initiative
Woodbury County, Iowa
www.woodburyorganics.com

Solar Tractor Conversion
The Community Farm of Ann Arbor, Michigan
www.communityfarmofaa.org

Sustainable Farmer online magazine
www.sustainablefarmer.com

SPIN Farming
www.spinfarming.com

Square Foot Gardening
www.squarefootgardening.com

Sustainable Growth Texas — Steve Diver
www.sustainablegrowthtexas.com

Tree People
2601 Mulholland Drive, Beverly Hills, CA 90210
Phone: (818) 753-4600
www.treepeople.org

University of Arkansas Applied Sustainability Center
www.sustainability.uark.edu

Urban Agriculture
www.ruaf.org

Urban Harvest
www.uharvest.org

Urban Homesteading
www.pathtofreedom.com

Woody Wodraska and Barbara Victoria Scott
www.soulmedicinejourney.com

Yale University Program in Agrarian Studies
www.yale.edu/agrarianstudies

Whole Systems Design
Moretown, VT
www.wholesystemsdesign.com

Worldwide Opportunities on Organic Farms (WWOOF — USA)
PO Box 432, Occidental, CA 95465 USA (831-425-FARM)
www.wwoofusa.org

Email Discussion Lists

SANET-MG: Sustainable Agriculture Research and Education — a discussion group
(listserv) for and about sustainable agriculture.
www.sare.org/about/sanetFAQ.htm

BDNow (Biodynamic farming & gardening)
www.bdnow.org
http://lists.envirolink.org/mailman/listinfo/bdnow

Back 40 — free online discussion group
www.Back40Forums.com

LocalHarvest
An organic and local food website. They maintain and routinely update nationwide
directory of small farms, farmers markets, and other local food sources.
www.localharvest.org

Permaculture course listings online.
www.Permaculture.Net

Permaculture — Discussion list for people who wish to design systems for
sustainable human habitats.
http://www.lists.ibiblio.org/mailman/listinfo/permaculture

Sustainable Agriculture mailing list:
http://lists.ibiblio.org/mailman/listinfo/sustag

Market Farming mailing list:
http://lists.ibiblio.org/mailman/listinfo/marketfarming

Seed Keepers — An email discussion list for people interested in saving seeds.
http://lists.ibiblio.org/mailman/listinfo/seedkeepers

FILMS:
"The Greenhorns" is a documentary film that explores the lives of America's young farming community—its spirit, practices, and needs.
www.thegreenhorns.net

"Homegrown" is a documentary film (2008) following the Dervaes family who run a small organic farm in the heart of Pasadena, California. While "living off the grid", they harvest over 6,000 pounds of produce on less than a quarter of an acre, make their own bio diesel, powering their computers with the help of solar panels.
www.homegrown-film.com

"The Organic Opportunity: Small Farms and Economic Development" is a 26-minute film telling the story of Woodbury County, Iowa, which has an economic development campaign centered on local organic agriculture.
www.chrisbedfordfilms.com

Small Farm Resources
"The Contrary Farmer" by Gene Logsdon (Chelsea Green Publishing) is a book for people starting up a farm on small acreage.

"Encyclopedia of Country Living" by Carla Emery, Sasquatch Books; Ninth edition (March 6, 2003)

"Five Acres and Independence" written well over a generation ago by Maurice Kains, still available and still bearing much useful information about living simply and well.

"Gardening When It Counts: Growing Food in Hard Times" by Steve Solomon (New Society Publishers, 2006). This book helps readers rediscover traditional low-input gardening methods. Designed for readers with no gardening experience.

"Grow It! — The Beginner's Complete In-Harmony-With-Nature Small Farm Guide — From Vegetable and Grain Growing to Livestock Care" by Richard W. Langer,1994, Noonday.

"The Have-More Plan: A Little Land — A Lot of Living" by Ed and Carolyn Robinson, Storey Books.

"How to Make $100,000 Farming 25 Acres: With Special Plans for Prospering on 10 to 200 Acres" by Booker T. Whatley. Ten practical steps from a small farm authority. Rodale Press, 1988.

"Making Your Small Farm Profitable" by Ron Macher, 1999, Storey Books, "The New Farmers' Market" by Vance Corum, Marcie Rosenzweig & Eric Gibson, 2001, New World Publishing. Written for farmers' market sellers, managers, market planners, and farmers' market community.

"Sell What You Sow! The Grower's Guide To Successful Produce Marketing" by Eric Gibson, 1993, New World Publishing.

"Small Farm Handbook" from the Small Farm Program, University of California –Davis, 1998. A practical guide on how to operate a small farm.

"Successful Small-Scale Farming" by Karl Schwenke, 1991, Storey Books.

"Small-Scale Grain Raising" by Gene Logsdon (Author), 1977. Rodale Books, Kutztown, PA.

Referenced Studies

The Benefits of Organic Agriculture, by Sandra Best. New Research and Studies, 2008.

The Biotechnology Bubble by Dr. Mae-Wan Ho. Joe Cummins, and Hartmut Meyer summarize the results of several experiments, trials and commercial releases of GMOs. The Ecologist. 1998.

CAFOs Uncovered: The Untold Costs of Confined Animal Feeding Operations, Union of Concerned Scientists, 2008.

Climate Change and Trace Gases, by James Hansen, M. Sato, P. Kharecha, G. Russell, D. Lea, M. Siddall, in Philosophical Transactions of the Royal Society, 2007.

CSA Home Delivery More Efficient
www.leopold.iastate.edu/news/newsreleases/2008/060608_csa.html

FAO Report says organic farming fights hunger, tackles climate change, good for farmers, consumers and the environment.
www.i-sis.org.uk/FAOPromotesOrganicAgriculture.php

International Commission on Education for Sustainable Development Practice, final report and global online classroom. www.mdp.ei.columbia.edu/?id=resourcecenter

A Silent Pandemic: Industrial Chemicals Are Impairing the Brain Development of Children Worldwide, by researchers at the Harvard School of Public Health and the Mount Sinai School of Medicine. The Lancet, 2006.

Organic Farming can Feed the World, by Yvette Perfecto and Catherine Badgley. Cambridge University Press, 2007.

Organic Yields Rival Conventional Yields for Some Crops. Agronomy Journal, 2008.

U.N. Panel Urges Changes to Feed Poor While Saving Environment, by Steven Erlander, *The New York Times*, April 16, 2008.

The Effects of Climate Change on Agriculture, Land Resources, Water Resources, and Biodiversity in the United States. U.S. Climate Change Science Program (CCSP) 2008 report.

Bibliography

Deep Gardening: Soul Lessons from 17 Gardens, by Woody Wodraska.
www.soulmedicinejourney.com

In Defense of Food, by Michael Pollan. Penguin, 2008.

Depletion and Abundance: Life on the New Home Front, by Sharon Astyk. New Society Publishers, 2008.

Farms of Tomorrow Revisited: Community Supported Farms — Farm Supported Communities, by Trauger Groh and Steven McFadden. Biodynamic Farming & Gardening Association, 1997.

Fifty Million Farmers — by Richard Heinberg. 26th Annual E. F. Schumacher Lectures, October 2006

Food Not Lawns: How to Turn your yard into a garden, and your neighborhood into a community by Heather Flores. Chelsea Green, 2006.

Farmer John's Cookbook: The real Dirt on Vegetables, by Farmer John Peterson and Angelic Organics. Gibbs Smith, Publisher, Layton, UT, 2006.

Four-Season Harvest: Organic vegetables from your home garden all year long, by Eliot Coleman. Chelsea Green Publishing, White River Junction, VT, 1992.

Gaia's Garden — A Guide to Home-Scale Permaculture by Toby Hemenway; Foreword by John Todd. Chelsea Green, 3rd edition, 2001.

Genetic Roulette: The Documented Health Risks of Genetically Engineered Foods, by Jeffrey Smith.

Going Local: Creating Self-Reliant Communities in a Global Age and The Small-Mart Revolution, by Michael H. Shuman. Kindle Book, 2000.

How to Grow More Vegetables, Fruits, Nuts, Berries, Grains, and Other Crops Than You Ever Thought Possible On Less Land Than You Can Imagine, by John Jeavons. Ten Speed Press, 2004.

Listening to the Land: Conversations About Nature, Culture and Eros by Derrick Jensen. Chelsea Green, 2004.

The New Organic Grower: A Master's Manual of Tools and Techniques for the Home and Market Gardener, by Eliot Coleman. Chelsea Green Publishing, White River Junction, VT, 1989.

The Omnivore's Dilemma, by Michael Pollan. Penguin, 2008.

Sharing the Harvest: A Guide to Community-Supported Agriculture, by Elizabeth Henderson with Robyn Van En. Chelsea Green Publishing, White River Junction, VT, 1999.

The Unsettling of America: Culture and Agriculture, by Wendell Berry. Sierra Club Books, San Francisco, CA, 1972.

The Way of Ignorance, and other essays, by Wendell Berry. Shoemaker & Hoard, Avalon Group, 2005.

A Nation of Farmers: Defeating the Food Crisis on American Soil, by Sharon Astyk and Aaron Newton. New Society Publishers, 2009.

Organic, Inc.: Natural Foods and How They Grew, by Samuel Fromartz. Harcourt, 2006.

The Party's Over: Oil, War and the Fate of Industrial Societies by Richard Heinberg. New Society, 2005.

Powerdown: Options and Actions for a Post-Carbon World by Richard Heinberg. New Society, 2004.

Peak Everything by Richard Heinberg. New Society, 2007.

Remaking the North American Food System: Strategies for Sustainability (Our Sustainable Future) by C. Clare Hinrichs and Thomas A. Lyson. University of Nebraska Press, 2008.

Revolution on the Range: The Rise of a New Ranch in the American West, by Courtney White. Island Press, 2008.

A Sand County Almanac, by Aldo Leopold. Ballentine Books, 1986.

Silent Spring by Rachel Carson. Houghton Mifflin, 1962.

Small-Scale Grain Raising by Gene Logsdon. Chelsea Green, 2008.

The Subsistence Perspective: Beyond the Globalized Economy, by Veronika Bennholt-Thomsen and Marie Mies. Zed Books, 2000.

The Way We Eat: Why Our Food Choices Matter, by Peter Singer and Jim Mason. Rodale Books, 2006.

Index

Made in the USA
Lexington, KY
04 December 2009